Lexington and Concord:

The First Shots of Freedom

How a Skirmish Ignited a Revolution

By

Blake Whitworth

This book is a work of nonfiction. Every effort has been made to ensure accuracy in the research, historical facts, and details presented. Some dialogue, scenes, and characterization have been selectively dramatized for narrative readability while maintaining historical integrity.

Printed in the United States of America

First Edition

This book is a work of nonfiction. Every effort has been made to ensure accuracy in the research, historical facts, and details presented. Some dialogue, scenes, and characterization have been selectively dramatized for narrative readability while maintaining historical integrity.

Printed in the United States of America

First Edition

Contents

Introduction

The morning of April 19, 1775, began with a chill that settled into the bones. Pale light crept across Lexington Green, catching on the dew that clung to every blade of grass. The quiet of dawn was broken only by the restless shuffling of boots and the low murmur of voices. On one side, a line of local militia—farmers, shopkeepers, and blacksmiths—stood with muskets in their hands, hearts pounding with uncertainty. Across the green, the red-coated ranks of British regulars advanced in measured steps, their faces set, their purpose clear but their nerves unsteady. For a long moment, the two sides faced each other in silence, each man wondering whether history would shift in the next breath. No one knew who would act first or what the cost would be.

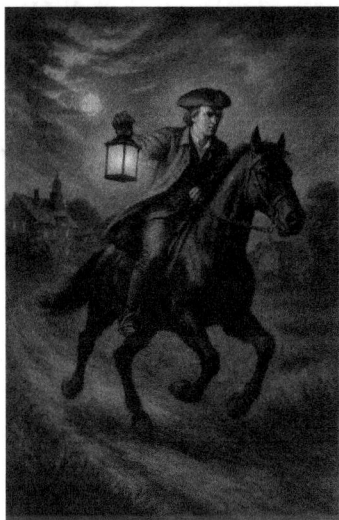

This book begins with that moment because it captures the heart of a mystery that has endured for nearly two and a half centuries: what exactly happened at Lexington and Concord? Who fired the first shot that morning, and how did a brief exchange of gunfire spark a revolution that would transform the world? These questions have fueled debate and speculation for generations. They remain at the root of how we remember the birth of the United States.

You may already know some of the stories, such as Paul Revere's midnight ride, as depicted herein, or the mysterious "shot heard 'round the world." These tales have become part of American legend, but they are often clouded by exaggeration or error. The journey you are about to take will begin with the years of rising tension leading up to 1775. You will see how arguments over taxes and rights gave way to mobilization and uncertainty.

We will follow the midnight rides of Revere, Dawes, and Prescott as they warned the countryside. We will walk with the militia and regulars as they march, hesitate, and finally clash at Lexington and Concord. The confusion and chaos of battle will give way to the aftermath—how communities mourned, debated, and began to see themselves as part of a new nation. The final chapters will trace the legacy of that day, showing how its lessons shape our understanding of conflict and courage even now. So, step into the story, challenge what you think you know, and join me in seeking the truth behind the legends. As shown above, we will discover how a tense standoff on a village green became the first shots of freedom. Then, follow me on to Concord, during that momentous day.

Chapter 1: Gathering Storms Seeds of Revolution in Massachusetts

In the early 1770s, unrest quietly permeated Massachusetts. Strolling through Lexington or Concord, you might have noticed neighbors huddled in discussion near meetinghouses, their glances turning nervously toward Boston. One Concord farmer jotted in his diary about rising sugar prices and the constant news coming from the city, while a Boston merchant lamented his financial losses and idle ships trapped by British taxes. Even children sensed something was amiss, overhearing passionate arguments in homes or at taverns where their parents gathered to debate. Across shops, fields, and homes, fundamental questions stirred: What right did Parliament have to interfere across the Atlantic? How much longer would people tolerate these burdens before demanding change?

Taxes, Tea, and Tumult – The Colonial Backlash to British Rule

After the costly French and Indian War, Britain sought to recover its debt through colonial taxation. The Sugar Act of 1764, taxing molasses and imports, directly threatened New England merchants; many turned to smuggling, but increased customs oversight heightened anxiety. Not only harbors, but shops in inland towns soon felt the strain as goods grew scarce and expensive.

The Stamp Act of 1765, taxing all paper documents and printed matter, unleashed more visible fury. In Boston, crowds protested under Liberty Trees, hung tax collectors in effigy, and the Sons of Liberty staged bold demonstrations. Mobs attacked officials' homes. This city-born anger soon spread—town meetings in rural Massachusetts echoed these sentiments, farmers and local leaders refusing compliance and signing petitions against Parliament. Though the act's 1766 repeal ended the tax, it left deep-seated mistrust. Parliament pressed on with more taxes. The Townshend Duties of 1767 added duties on glass, paper, paint, and tea. This time, resistance took the form of unified boycotts. Merchants agreed not to import British goods; families embraced homespun cloth and herbal teas.

Across Massachusetts, communities found pride in self-reliance and sacrifice, symbolized by Liberty Poles rising on greens. Newspapers published names of those who honored or broke the boycotts, reinforcing local accountability.

Tensions climaxed with the Boston Tea Party in December 1773, when disguised Patriots dumped tea into the harbor. News spread quickly—even far from Boston, people wrote in disbelief about the event. The British response—the closure of Boston's port—shocked all of Massachusetts. Commerce in Boston stalled as ships lay idle; wharves fell silent.

Surrounding towns did not ignore Boston's plight. Town records reveal widespread support as communities gathered money and supplies—grain, livestock, and other relief—

sending aid to the city. Small villages and parishes joined in, forging tighter bonds between city and countryside. These collective efforts transformed scattered protests into a regional struggle. In meetinghouses and churchyards, people rallied behind Boston both as an act of charity and defiance.

New forms of resistance emerged: Committees were formed to coordinate aid and enforce boycotts, and Liberty Poles became rallying points for Patriot gatherings. In taverns throughout Massachusetts, heated debates over taxes and self-government grew more frequent. Rural letters and diaries reveal the emotional toll of the crisis— fear for livelihoods mixed with cautious optimism that steadfastness might secure future freedom.

One Concord farmer wrote to his cousin in Acton about intense discussions at Wright's Tavern: "Some say we must submit or be ruined; others claim no man in England knows our hardships nor has any right to rule us so." In Lexington, a blacksmith's diary recounted late-night neighborhood arguments—at once lamenting lost business and expressing pride in resisting British goods.

By spring 1775, these British policies had done more than cause economic pain—they had sparked a powerful awakening. Each new act intensified resentment and encouraged greater collective action. Aid for Boston became a symbol of shared identity; Liberty Poles were declarations of allegiance; even private correspondence was charged with talk of rights and responsibilities. Across

Massachusetts, change was no longer being endured—it was being prepared for, with a society uniting toward inevitable conflict.

Reflection Section: Voices from the Towns

Imagine yourself in Lexington or Concord at this time— would you join the boycotts and risk your livelihood? Would you send food to support Boston? Write a brief note as an apprentice or farmer in 1774: What would you say about your hopes and fears?

The Powder Alarm of 1774 – Testing the Colonial Resolve

September 1, 1774, dawned humid and thick with late-summer haze over the outskirts of Boston. As the city slowly awakened, British soldiers quietly marched toward the Charlestown Powder House, a stout octagonal structure on a hill north of the city. Their orders were simple but provocative: remove the gunpowder stored there before local militias could claim it. The operation began with stealth—no fanfare, no public announcement.

Yet word of the removal did not stay secret for long. By midmorning, a handful of laborers and passersby spotted British carts leaving the powder house, escorted by regulars. Within an hour, rumors began to swirl through taverns and markets: "The redcoats have seized all the powder!" "The war is starting!" "They've fired on townspeople near Cambridge!" Fact blurred rapidly into fiction, and with each retelling, the alarm grew more frantic.

The countryside responded with astonishing speed. Bells tolled from village steeples; alarm guns boomed in the distance. Riders mounted swift horses and dashed along dirt roads, spreading the warning from Boston's edges into Middlesex County and beyond. In Lexington, Concord, and dozens of small towns, church bells clanged in urgent patterns. Men left plows in furrows and tools on benches, grabbing muskets and powder horns before hurrying toward their muster points. The sense of emergency was palpable— fathers called for sons, neighbors rapped on doors, and entire communities surged toward Boston in a spontaneous wave. Within hours, thousands of militiamen were marching toward the city, some convinced they would find blood already spilled in the streets.

This surge of bodies and nerves demonstrated the effectiveness of colonial communication networks. Riders did not travel alone; as each passed through a village, local messengers fanned out in all directions. Simple codes— three quick bell tolls or volleys—signaled nearby towns to arm themselves.

News moved with incredible speed for the era, fueled by face-to-face warnings and shared urgency. False details often traveled faster than the truth. One rumor insisted that British soldiers had killed several Bostonians; another claimed warships were shelling the harbor. These fabrications were not deliberate lies but the natural byproduct of panic and outrage, amplified by every retelling.

In Concord, a particularly vivid scene unfolded as militia officers gathered at Wright's Tavern. Town records note frantic debates—should they march directly to Boston or await more news? Some leaders urged caution, suspecting exaggeration; others feared delay might mean missing the opening shots of war. The crowd outside grew restless, demanding action. Similar scenes played out in Lexington and dozens of villages. Even older men too frail for battle arrived at muster grounds, determined to offer what help they could.

The British authorities watched this mobilization with mingled shock and apprehension. General Gage, governor of Massachusetts and commander of British forces in Boston, had intended the powder seizure as a routine precaution. The overwhelming colonial response left him momentarily paralyzed—he issued hasty reassurances that no violence had occurred, urging local leaders to stand down their militias. Meanwhile, Loyalist observers grew anxious, questioning whether British authority could be maintained without provoking outright rebellion.

Local Patriot leaders worked feverishly to prevent violence once it became clear that no shots had been fired and no blood had been spilled. Clergymen calmed congregations with careful explanations; respected elders addressed crowds from town greens, urging restraint until facts emerged. In Cambridge, where militias had gathered in force by the afternoon, cooler heads prevailed—some called for negotiation rather than confrontation. By evening, as reliable messengers confirmed there had been no battle or massacre, most militiamen reluctantly returned home, weary but relieved.

Despite its anticlimactic end, the Powder Alarm marked a turning point in colonial readiness. Towns recognized how quickly confusion could ignite mass mobilization—and how easily misinformation could spiral out of control. In the weeks that followed, militia captains revised muster procedures; some established stricter rosters and clearer chains of command. Powder magazines were relocated or hidden more carefully, and towns conducted more frequent drills to ensure discipline. Leaders reflected quietly on how close they had come to war that day.

The Powder Alarm exposed both the strengths and vulnerabilities of colonial society—its unity, its capacity for swift action, but also its susceptibility to fear and rumor. The lessons learned would echo loudly in April 1775, when real gunfire would replace false alarms.

The Committees of Correspondence – Spreading the Fire

The Committees of Correspondence formed the backbone of colonial unity in the turbulent months before open conflict. Born from necessity, these groups first took shape in Boston, where local leaders realized that isolated protests would falter unless towns coordinated their resistance. Samuel Adams, James Otis, and Joseph Warren—names still spoken with reverence—drafted the original call to action in late 1772, their words echoing through the streets and alleys of Boston before spreading to rural parishes and farmsteads in Middlesex County. But it was not only the famous who drove this transformation. With a single circular letter, the Boston committee invited every town to appoint its own correspondents and respond not just with sympathy but with practical cooperation. These letters, carefully copied by hand, traveled from village to village, riding in the saddlebags of travelers or passed across tavern tables, each one a spark landing on dry tinder.

Circular letters often read like manifestos but carried the everyday language of neighbors—a mix of grievances, warnings, and urgent invitations. One famous example sent after a British crackdown in Boston outlined not only violations of rights but demanded that each town join in a "constant and free communication of our sentiments." In Concord, committee members gathered at the courthouse to read aloud these appeals, then drafted their own statements of support and concern. Even modest towns like Lincoln or Acton responded eagerly, sending delegates or answering with affirming votes at town meetings. This web of correspondence grew denser each week, knitting together communities once separated by distance and suspicion.

The committees became engines of both information and resistance. They investigated rumors with unflinching resolve, sometimes summoning neighbors suspected of Loyalist sympathies for questioning. In Lexington, for example, a well-known innkeeper faced public scrutiny after rumors emerged that he had provided food to British soldiers traveling through the area.

Local committees did not act as mere busybodies; they recorded statements, cross-examined witnesses, and compiled evidence before reporting their findings to the wider community. Sometimes their work bordered on intimidation—Loyalists risked having their names published in broadsides pinned to meetinghouse doors or posted at market squares. These public notices urged townspeople to remain alert and to shun those seen as betraying the Patriot cause.

Broadsides—large printed sheets—became the primary means for communicating both encouragement and warning. One broadside published in Concord warned against "the insidious designs of our enemies" and called upon every household to remain vigilant. Another listed merchant who had honored boycott agreements alongside those who had broken ranks, a practice that often led to heated confrontations in shops or at Sunday services. Even church congregations were drawn into political debates as ministers read committee statements from pulpits or hosted meetings after worship. In some cases, committees dispatched members to other towns to share strategies or mediate disputes, further entwining the fate of each community with its neighbors'.

The work of these committees was not carried out by grand statesmen alone but by ordinary men whose names rarely appear in textbooks. In Lexington, Jonas Clarke—a minister whose parsonage would soon serve as headquarters for militia leaders—acted as both mediator and correspondent, penning letters that balanced caution with resolve. John Hancock's influence loomed large from Boston, but it was local figures like Deacon Joseph Robbins of Acton or Dr. Samuel Prescott of Concord who carried news on horseback during emergencies. In reading their correspondence today, we glimpse not only political strategy but genuine anxiety—a sense that the smallest errors could endanger families and friends.

Committee work touched every aspect of daily life. Boycotts required careful coordination; committee members visited shops to ensure imported goods remained off shelves and encouraged alternatives like homespun cloth or herbal teas. They organized town meetings on short notice, sometimes gathering crowds late into the evening to debate letters received that morning. In one recorded instance from Sudbury, a merchant who ignored boycott rules found himself before a committee hearing, facing not only reprimand but social isolation as townspeople took their business elsewhere. Church congregations were not immune; ministers who failed to speak against British policies risked losing support or being replaced by more zealous voices.

This network fostered a sense of shared destiny rarely seen before in colonial America. Petty disputes faded as the committees' work forced townsfolk to confront larger questions about loyalty and responsibility. Every circular letter read aloud at a meeting became a call to vigilance; every broadside posted in a tavern reminded people that their actions mattered beyond their own fences. The Committees of Correspondence transformed isolated pockets of defiance into an organized movement, making it possible for Massachusetts to speak—and eventually act—with one voice as the crisis approached.

Loyalists, Patriots, and Fence-Sitters – Divided Communities

The towns and villages of Massachusetts in 1774 and early 1775 were not painted in patriotic unity. Instead, lines of allegiance twisted through every crossroads, down every lane, and even across supper tables. In Lexington, the story of a family divided by the rising storm was not uncommon. One brother, a joiner by trade, had thrown his lot with the local committee, attending meetings and voicing support for resistance. His sister, married to a merchant who did brisk business with British officers in Boston, urged caution and worried that reckless actions would ruin their livelihood. Their father, a church deacon, tried to keep peace at home but found his household echoing the larger discord of the town. Such fissures ran through many families—sometimes quietly, sometimes erupting into accusations or icy silences.

Social pressure shaped these divisions as much as politics did. Patriots—those openly supporting resistance—wielded powerful tools to enforce conformity. Suspected Loyalists faced public humiliation: sometimes neighbors nailed warning posters to their doors, or crowds gathered to force apologies on the meetinghouse steps. In certain cases, offenders were "ridden out" on rails or subjected to mock trials in tavern yards. Even children took part, taunting classmates whose parents were rumored to favor the Crown. Those branded as Loyalists often saw business dry up or found themselves shunned at church services. The threat of ostracism was real and could fracture friendships built over a lifetime.

Motivations for loyalty or dissent rarely followed a simple pattern. Economic interests played a central part—Boston merchants with contracts from London had much to lose if trade collapsed, while inland farmers who bartered with neighbors felt less exposed. Religion held sway as well. Anglican ministers, whose pay sometimes came directly from England, tended toward caution or silence, while Congregationalist preachers spoke with fire about liberty and rights. Past grievances colored decisions; a shopkeeper denied a lucrative contract by the town committee might suddenly adopt Loyalist sympathies, while those embittered by British soldiers' conduct in Boston nursed patriotic resolve. Fear lingered at the edge of every calculation: fear of property loss, fear for personal safety, fear that war would sweep away everything familiar.

Several individuals from the region illustrate the complexity of allegiance. A Concord merchant who once hosted British officers at his home turned Patriot after soldiers failed to pay their bills. In Lincoln, a respected schoolmaster tried for months to hold himself aloof from both sides—he wanted only to teach—but eventually drew scrutiny after an offhand remark at a church supper was misconstrued as Loyalist sympathy. A clergyman in Bedford preached reconciliation until members of his congregation accused him of cowardice and pressed him to declare his stance. These cases reveal how social standing and reputation could shift overnight depending on perceived loyalty.

Fence-sitters—those who hesitated, avoided public declarations, or tried to remain neutral—found themselves increasingly squeezed as tensions escalated. Town meeting minutes from the period record repeated calls for "all able-bodied men" to pledge support for local defense committees. Some residents offered vague assurances or pledged only limited support, hoping to avoid trouble no matter which side prevailed. Diarists recorded the anxiety of walking a careful line: one wrote that he "wished neither King nor Congress ill" but felt "the press of neighbors' eyes." The cost of indecision grew heavier with each passing week.

Communal preparations for conflict exposed these fractures in sharp relief. When towns called for militia enlistment, debate often erupted over who could be trusted with arms and who might betray secrets to British authorities. In some villages, men suspected of Loyalist leanings were quietly left off muster rolls or excluded from nighttime drills. Local defense planning became fraught as committee leaders weighed loyalty against necessity—could an able-bodied man be denied a musket on suspicion alone? Families who tried to keep their heads down found themselves visited by committees demanding pledges or explanations.

Yet even in this climate of suspicion and pressure, many clung to hopes for reconciliation or simply waited for events to clarify which path would prove safest. The fence-sitter's lot remained uncertain and uncomfortable. Some would eventually be swept up in the tide of events—pressed into service, forced into exile, or finally declaring for one side when neutrality became impossible. In Massachusetts on the eve of war, unity was more aspiration than fact; division was the daily reality threading through every decision and conversation.

"Minute Men" Muster – Building the Colonial Militia

The rise of the "minute men" marked a new chapter in the story of Massachusetts resistance. Unlike the old militias, which had long served as local defense but met only a few times each year, this new force demanded more from its members. In October 1774, the Massachusetts Provincial Congress voted to create "minute companies"—groups of volunteers pledged to be ready at a moment's notice, hence their striking name. Each town was to select about one quarter of its able-bodied men for this special duty. These were not just any volunteers; they were chosen for their reliability, their speed, and their willingness to drop everything for the alarm. The Provincial Congress set strict muster requirements: minute men must practice regularly, keep arms and powder at hand, and promise to assemble "on the shortest warning." They were expected to gather within thirty minutes of an alarm—a demand that set them apart from traditional militia who might need hours or even days to mobilize.

The men who filled these ranks came from every walk of life. Some were barely past boyhood, others already gray with years of hard labor. In Lexington, you would have found John Parker, a farmer and former soldier whose experience made him a natural leader; nearby stood Prince Estabrook, an enslaved man serving his community on the same green as his neighbors. Concord's rolls listed blacksmiths, carpenters, cobblers, and innkeepers—men like Samuel Barrett, who left his forge behind at the sound of the drum, and Amos Barrett, a young laborer eager to prove himself. Each minute man balanced the needs of his family with the demands of duty. Some left behind aging parents or wives expecting children; others shouldered the hopes of younger siblings. Their motivations varied: a sense of justice, loyalty to friends, fear for home, or hope for a better future. Yet all shared the risk of sudden violence and the pride of standing with their neighbors.

Training routines were both communal and rigorous. Muster days brought excitement and nervous anticipation. On appointed mornings—sometimes announced by the clang of the church bell—men gathered on the village green, muskets slung over shoulders, powder horns clinking at their belts. Older officers marched them through drills: forming lines two deep, stepping in rhythm, learning to load and fire in unison. Commands echoed across open fields and between gravestones in churchyards pressed into service for practice. The youngest watched and learned, itching for their turn. Practice was not just about marching but about speed—minute men had to assemble swiftly, respond to orders without confusion, and stand ready for whatever threat loomed.

Weapon storage posed challenges. Most men kept muskets close at hand—hanging above hearths or tucked behind doors—while powder and ball were jealously guarded against dampness or theft. Towns maintained public stores in locked magazines or hidden cellars, but personal stockpiles mattered most when alarms sounded. Powder was precious; shortages loomed over every drill. Communities appointed powder keepers to ration supplies and ensure no one was left empty-handed in a crisis. Ball was cast at home from salvaged metal—old pewter mugs or broken tools melted down and poured into simple molds.

The process of supplying and equipping minutemen demanded cooperation. Women sewed cartridge boxes or knit warm stockings for cold mornings on guard; children gathered scrap lead for bullets or watched younger siblings while fathers drilled. On muster day, neighbors traded stories as they cleaned muskets or compared powder horns, sharing advice on the best way to prime a pan or aim down a smoky barrel. Drills became social events as much as military preparation—a chance to reaffirm bonds and share laughter when nerves ran high.

Yet beneath this sense of community ran undercurrents of anxiety. Letters written home by those training with the minute companies often reveal a blend of pride and worry.

One Concord father wrote to his cousin about the "great stir in town," describing both his satisfaction in watching his eldest son drill and his fear "that blood may be spilt before long." Another young man confided to his brother that he felt "a trembling in my hand when I take up my musket," unsure whether he would stand firm when real danger arrived. Oral traditions recall neighbors urging one another not to falter should the alarm come in earnest—a mixture of bravado and real fear.

The uncertainty was real and pressing. No one could predict if or when British troops might march out from Boston, nor what form the first confrontation would take. Still, each week spent practicing, each ball cast or cartridge box stitched, brought ordinary people closer to readiness. The minutemen's experience was shaped as much by duty and pride as it was by sleepless nights and whispered doubts over supper tables.

Infographic: Anatomy of a Minute Man

[If you had this book in print: See the illustrated breakdown showing a typical minute man's gear—musket, powder horn, cartridge box, homespun coat—and the timeline for assembling after an alarm.]

British Eyes on Concord – Intelligence, Spies, and Secret Arms

During the winter of 1774 and early 1775, Massachusetts became a battleground of intelligence. Fearing the growing stockpiles of colonial arms, British officials in Boston—

especially Governor General Thomas Gage—watched with growing alarm as rumors swirled of secret cannon, gunpowder, and musket balls being moved at night to barns and cellars throughout Middlesex County. The reports made Concord a particular concern, with its reputation as a major storehouse threatening to arm Patriot resistance if open conflict erupted.

To get reliable information, Gage built a web of spies and Loyalist sympathizers—merchants who frequented the countryside and regulars in local taverns who blended in among the farmers. Informants reported every odd wagon and secret gathering. Some even used coded correspondence; one Loyalist from Acton sent weekly coded messages about activity in Concord, sometimes overstating the threat. Still, these reports convinced Gage that immediate action was called for. Patriots, aware of spying, became cautious. They used hushed voices, coded language—calling arms "tools" or powder "seed corn"—to obscure their intent in person and in letters.

British officer John Howe's civilian-reconnaissance missions became well known during these months. Disguised, he wandered Concord, counting cannon carriages and peeking into barns under innocuous pretenses. His notes charted stores and militia strength, but Patriot locals were adept at misdirecting him—showing only empty sheds or leading him away from concealed magazines. Patriot stores were often emptied and relocated on short notice, eluding British surveillance.

Both sides developed and adapted clever tactics. Patriots relocated arms at unpredictable intervals, splitting up stockpiles among farms or even burying powder and cannon under haystacks and inside wells. When British scouts were rumored to be near, the militia organized night work parties to load and secretly disperse munitions along back roads. Only a trusted few ever knew the real locations, maintaining tight security even within their own towns.

Coded correspondence was essential for the Patriots. Letters between militia captains and Boston leaders especially avoided direct references to arms, relying instead on agreed phrasings or symbols. Interception posed a real risk; a single careless word could expose many. One Concord deacon wrote about "the shipment received at the old barn," while a nearby town cryptically reported "the oxen being well-fed," meaning powder was secure.

British intelligence was heavily reliant on Loyalists who took great personal risks by operating between enemy lines; they listened closely at public gatherings, spied on militia drills, and kept Gage's command updated. Their sometimes-exaggerated reports still spurred British planning. Warnings of cannon in Concord meetinghouse or powder near Barrett's farm spurred the expedition that would march on April 19.

Colonial counterintelligence became equally vital. Towns invented informal warning systems—such as patterns of bell-ringing or lanterns—to alert people if strangers or British agents appeared. Women often acted as road watchers, discreetly signaling neighbors about the presence of suspected spies. Even schoolchildren helped as secret messengers, their errands hiding pressed warnings.

These subtle maneuvers built tension on both sides. General Gage's final Concord orders came after months of incomplete but persistent intelligence; he believed removing colonial arms would break resistance. For colonists, each rumor of a spy or Loyalist betrayal heightened secrecy and vigilance. Patriots mastered the arts of hiding, code-speak, and healthy suspicion—even among neighbors.

In this shadowy contest, both sides grew wiser in deception and security. By April 1775, confidence was elusive; caches could be compromised, messengers intercepted at any time. Yet this climate bred agility and alertness in the Patriots, preparing them for the moment when these games would explode into open conflict.

The tension peaked days before April 19: rumors flew about imminent British marches, traitors, and freshly betrayed hiding spots around Concord. Patriot and Redcoat moved cautiously, uncertain whether the other was ahead or behind. The British regulars marched out at dawn on April 19, not fully assured by their intelligence, aware that the Patriots may well stay a step ahead.

In these high-stakes games of nerve and cunning, the fate of the rebellion balanced—one hidden cache and coded message at a time.

Chapter 2: The Night Before Riders, Rumors, and Alarms

Paul Revere, William Dawes, and Samuel Prescott – Mapping the Midnight Rides

Midnight across Boston's outskirts hums with tension. Paul Revere stands by the Charles River, awaiting news. Two lanterns briefly gleam atop Old North Church—British regulars will cross by water. Revere launches his silent rowboat journey past British patrols, landing safely at Charlestown. Borrowing a Patriot horse, he rides through tense, familiar lanes, his first stop at Richard Devens' home for vital British intel. Without delay, Revere races toward Lexington: Samuel Adams and John Hancock must be warned.

Simultaneously, William Dawes leaves Boston by the more arduous, southern land route via Boston Neck, past British posts. With forged papers, Dawes passes the guards after a tense moment and rides on through Roxbury, Brookline, and Cambridge. Though longer, his route offers critical surprise, as British forces expect trouble from the north. Dawes battles muddy spring roads and the threat of interception, but presses on, discreetly spreading alarm at each crossroads and tavern.

Revere and Dawes reach Lexington just before dawn. At Reverend Jonas Clarke's parsonage, they deliver urgent warnings to Hancock and Adams. Nearby, Buckman Tavern is alive with local militia preparing to act. Here, Dr.

Samuel Prescott, a Concord physician, joins by chance. The three—Revere, Dawes, Prescott—form the next link in the warning chain, setting out for Concord down winding roads flanked by stone walls and spring orchards.

Obstacles quickly appear. British patrols scour the countryside, hoping to stop such alarms. Near Menotomy, patrols confront them: Revere is captured and held at gunpoint, ending his ride abruptly. Dawes escapes immersion but is thrown from his horse and must go to ground in the darkness. Only Prescott, leveraging his local knowledge and quick thinking, flees into wooded pastures and avoids capture.

Prescott's ride becomes vital. He rushes along the Bay Road, waking homes and taverns—Hartwell Tavern included—spreading urgent news. Each house or inn becomes a crucial relay point: lanterns shine in windows; families mobilize; militia captains coordinate further relays deeper into the countryside.

These rides were not solo heroics but highly coordinated teamwork. Each rider relied on local support: Patriots readying fresh horses, hiding riders or mounts, supplying food, or helping to pass messages. People listened for approaching hooves, armed themselves, and prepared their homes to serve the alarm effort. Prescott's ride through Lincoln into Concord depended on such cooperation— farmers meeting him at crossroads, relaying the alarm further west to Sudbury and Acton.

Improvisation was common. Captured, Revere misleads his guards about militia strength. Dawes finds help after his accident at a farmhouse. Prescott's intimate familiarity with the landscape helps him avoid capture and continue his warning mission. The system functioned because everyone knew their roles and trusted each other.

While Revere, Dawes, and Prescott became best known, the alarm system depended on a community-wide network. Many more, like Israel Bissell (who raced toward Worcester), or Sybil Ludington (later repeating such midnight rides in New York), joined these efforts. Women played essential roles: keeping watch, supplying information, and hiding riders or horses.

Alarm Riders Spread the Word – The Human Relay Network

On that tense April night, an intricate network of alarm riders stretched across Massachusetts, delivering urgent warnings that few realize included many more than just the famous names. In nearly every hamlet, back road, and remote farm, communities depended on a carefully planned system: one rider delivered the message—"The regulars are out!"—and another immediately took off to the next location. Patriots had established these relays ahead of time, choosing reliable messengers and mapping out the fastest routes. Warnings spread by word of mouth at crossroads, with others rousing neighbors by banging on shutters or doors until lanterns flickered on. Each new messenger pushed the alarm farther, stopping only to hand off the message, so news traveled much faster than British troops could march.

Pre-arranged signals supported the riders' efforts. The Old North Church in Boston used two lanterns from its steeple—one if the British came by land, two if by water—to quickly inform Patriot watchers across the river. In more distant towns, other signals took over: the ringing of church bells, which called men from their beds or fields, or three rapid gunshots to warn of immediate danger. These were not random noises; they triggered a coordinated response, sending church sextons, tavern keepers, and farmers into action.

Throughout this sprawling network, countless unsung individuals played vital roles. William Diamond, just sixteen, was Lexington's drummer. On Lexington Green, his steady drumming signaled the call-to-arms and brought order at a chaotic moment. Farther west, Israel Bissell rode swiftly from Watertown toward Worcester and beyond, covering nearly forty miles that first day, before fresh riders continued his warning on toward Springfield and New York. In many towns, local leaders—whether schoolmasters, deacons, or respected tradesmen—joined the relay, using their influence to persuade even doubtful neighbors of the real threat.

The speed of the network was astonishing. News reached Acton before midnight, so Captain Isaac Davis could ready his men for a dawn march to Concord. In Bedford, church bells rang until families gathered outside, startled from sleep, as fathers prepared for battle. Sudbury's alarm came in time for Captain John Nixon to organize his men before sunrise. These were not isolated events; diaries and letters describe wakes from sudden knocking or shouting in the night, families hastily assembling weapons and supplies, and women bundling food or clothing for the men going to fight.

Firsthand accounts capture the fear and resolve of the moment: a Bedford woman recalled waking to her husband's urgent voice, "The British are marching; I must go," and watching him kiss their sleeping children goodbye as he left with his musket. In Sudbury, a young apprentice wrote of his master rousing everyone to spread the word. Within hours, entire communities mobilized: neighbors cared for one another's children, and elders tended animals left behind in the rush.

This mobilization came from months of planning and shared commitment. Towns had practiced alarms before— most notably during the Powder Alarm of 1774—and refined their responses from those experiences. Riders always had backup: if one was stopped or fell, another was ready to continue. Flexibility and discipline ensured that no single failure could stop the spread of news.

For a few crucial hours, this human network erased distance. Isolated farms were as connected as busy town centers. Lanterns glowed in windows, bells echoed through fields and woods, and gunshots cracked the night, answered by distant echoes. Every sound was both a warning and a rallying call, uniting communities in action.

Even after the first shots at Lexington Green at dawn, the alarm network kept working. Riders who started before midnight continued, despite exhaustion and confusion, to towns like Framingham, Marlborough, and Groton. By the time most British soldiers turned to retreat, the entire region was already mobilized. The events that unfolded were more than a military response—they showed how ordinary people, connected by purpose, could outpace professional armies with determination, communication, and unity.

Myths and Realities of the Midnight Rides – Separating Legend from Fact

Few American stories are as entrenched as Paul Revere's midnight ride. The common narrative has Revere riding alone, shouting, "The British are coming!" as he alerts sleeping colonists. This vivid, enduring image dominates how most people recall that night. However, primary sources and research paint a much more complex picture, involving a network of people and very different warnings from those in the legend.

First, consider the iconic phrase: "The British are coming!" Revere almost certainly never said this. At the time, most colonists still identified as British, so this warning would have been confusing. Revere used more precise warnings such as "The regulars are out!" or "The regulars are coming out!" to refer specifically to the British soldiers—the redcoats stationed in Boston who posed a threat to colonial leaders and arm stores. He and other alarm riders tailored their language for urgency and clarity.

Another persistent myth is that Revere rode alone, single-handedly spreading the alarm. In fact, the night's warning was a coordinated group effort. William Dawes left Boston on a different route, and Samuel Prescott joined after Lexington. Dozens—and very likely hundreds—of local men and boys also carried the news, some on horseback, and others on foot, fanning out across Middlesex County and beyond. Many messengers remain unnamed in the historical record. The "lone hero" tale oversimplifies what was actually a community-wide response.

Nor did the system work flawlessly. Some riders were delayed or captured; some people slept through knocks and had to be awakened a second time. Not every town sprang into instant action, but overall, most communities responded quickly enough to muster thousands of militia before the British reached Concord. The process was messy but remarkably effective given the circumstances.

Why, then, is Paul Revere remembered above all others? Early histories included many riders and informants, but in 1861, Henry Wadsworth Longfellow's poem "Paul Revere's Ride" turned Revere into an icon. Longfellow's poem crafted a simple, resonant story of courage, deliberately blending facts for dramatic effect. The poem gained particular popularity during the Civil War, when Americans were eager for revolutionary heroes. By centering the narrative on one man's ride, Longfellow's version traded complexity for memorable myth.

Longfellow's influence shaped education and public memory. Early schoolbooks relied heavily on his poem, and generations of children grew up memorizing lines that described Revere as the solitary sentinel of liberty. This national story overshadowed New England's more detailed local histories, which remembered Dawes, Prescott, and many unnamed riders as equally critical in spreading the alarm.

Regional storytelling continues to shape commemorations. In places like Lexington and Concord, markers and statues honor a range of local riders. Town records recount neighbors—men and sometimes boys—who ran through the night to carry the alarm. Outside New England, though, it's largely Revere's name that survives, thanks to both Longfellow and the appeal of a straightforward, heroic narrative.

Historical documents provide a messier and richer story. Revere's own testimony after the battles describes warning local militia leaders: "I alarmed almost every house till I got to Lexington." He named other riders and recounted being captured by British patrols, far from the uninterrupted dash to Concord that legend suggests. Local histories note names of men who warned Acton, Sudbury, and neighboring towns, describing their chaotic journeys and the confusion of the night.

Myth vs Fact Sidebar

Myth: Paul Revere rode alone, yelling, "The British are coming!"

Fact: Many riders were involved, and phrases like "The regulars are out!" were actually used.

Myth: Longfellow's poem is literal history.

Fact: The poem simplifies and dramatizes the events, turning a team effort into a solo ride.

Recognizing these distinctions brings us closer to the truth of what happened when the alarms first sounded. The real story highlights collective action: a large, coordinated network of riders, a patchwork of communities rallying in uncertainty, and a warning system rooted in trust and mutual responsibility—not solitary heroics. This understanding honors the many ordinary people whose quick decisions and bravery shaped the course of history.

British March Orders – Gage's Gamble and Secret Dispatches

On April 18, 1775, within the tense walls of Boston, General Thomas Gage confronted a decision with far-reaching consequences. Months of escalating conflict between Parliament and the colonists had left Massachusetts on a knife's edge, with militias drilling openly and Patriot leaders' defiance mounting. Gage saw the colonial arms stockpiled in Concord as a direct threat to British control. He crafted a plan balancing daring and secrecy: send a swift, elite force to seize or destroy the munitions before open rebellion erupted.

Gage's orders were both clear and intensely secretive. That evening, he discreetly summoned Lieutenant Colonel Francis Smith and Major John Pitcairn. The written orders instructed Smith to lead a select group of light infantry and grenadiers—chosen for speed and intimidation—along with Pitcairn's Marines. Their route was through Lexington, where Adams and Hancock might be hiding. The mission: confiscate or destroy arms and powder, arrest leading rebels if possible, and do it before the countryside could be warned. With secrecy paramount, the regulars were to depart late and reach Concord by dawn, ideally before Patriot riders could signal danger.

Every aspect of the preparations emphasized secrecy. Gage and his officers relayed instructions only to trusted sergeants, withholding information from most soldiers until the final moments. Whaleboats waited covertly at Back Bay to transport troops over the Charles River to Cambridge. Men were ordered to carry only essentials, march quietly, and avoid drawing attention—no drums or fifes, and small groups left barracks separately to avoid arousing Boston's Patriot observers.

The whaleboat crossing was a tense, silent operation. Troops, muskets at their sides and bayonets sheathed, slipped across the river in clusters, speaking in hushed tones. Some soldiers were unsure of their destination; others sensed the unusual urgency. Officers surveilled discipline, insisting on silence and discretion as the units assembled on the Cambridge shore to regroup before marching west.

Despite Gage's careful planning, confusion and delays crept in. Logistical issues arose: several whaleboats lagged behind due to shifting tides and shoreline obstacles. Troops grew restless in the chilly night as they waited for the full column to assemble. Organizing Smith's command in darkness proved difficult and wasted valuable time, sparking grumbling over unclear orders and incomplete supplies. Some feared, even before the march began, that the vital secrecy was slipping away.

British intelligence faltered. Loyalist informants warned Gage that colonial spies carefully monitored every troop movement in Boston. Gage underestimated the Patriots' communication networks and the thoroughness of their surveillance. For days, many Patriots suspected a British march was imminent. Snatched conversations, officers' hurried messages, and soldiers departing after dark all heightened local alarm.

Inside the ranks, anxiety simmered beneath a surface of discipline. Letters from junior officers to family described feeling lost, uncertain of both orders and destinations, and aware of increasing hostility in the countryside. Some wrote of boredom and discomfort during the delays, while others confessed trepidation about marching into potentially hostile villages. Private accounts expressed more doubt and fear than the confident tone of official reports.

Loyalist informants, likewise, watched events with a mixture of hope and dread. Some clung to the belief that a firm, rapid show of force might restore British authority without violence. Others, noting the whispers and hurried movements of the night, suspected secrecy had already failed—and that colonial alarm riders would easily outpace British speed.

For the British officers, tension was palpable. Gage was keenly aware that a misstep might not only cost arms but also trigger outright war. Smith and Pitcairn tried to bolster their men's morale but knew unpredictability awaited beyond Cambridge. The diverse possibilities ahead ranged from a quiet seizure of arms to a bloody confrontation with hidden militia.

Every decision—each secretive order, each delay at the river—contributed to what would happen at Lexington and Concord come sunrise. The British regulars set forth draped in secrecy and hope for surprise, but uncertainty clung to them as much as the Charles River's drifting night mist.

Colonial Spies in Boston – Watching the Redcoats' Every Move

Boston, under British occupation in April 1775, was a city where every movement carried weight. Patriot leaders understood that information, not just muskets, could tip the balance. At the center of this invisible contest stood Dr. Joseph Warren, a respected physician and passionate advocate for colonial rights. He built an intelligence network as complex as any battlefield formation. Warren worked quietly, organizing a trusted circle of informants drawn from all walks of life—dockworkers, shopkeepers, servants in Loyalist homes, even sympathetic British soldiers. These individuals risked everything to observe troop gatherings, overhear officers' conversations, and note shipments of supplies or sudden disappearances of key Redcoat units.

Gathering intelligence required both subtlety and ingenuity. Many informants used coded language in their notes—a simple phrase about "unusual guests at supper" might signal British officers conferring late into the night; "the river's busy" could indicate troop movement toward the water. Dr. Warren and his closest confidants met in discreet locations, including crowded taverns where whispered words blended with the clatter of mugs and laughter. Sometimes, they gathered in private back rooms of apothecaries or behind locked church doors after dark. Trusted messengers—often young boys or women less likely to draw suspicion—carried these coded messages tucked inside loaves of bread, sewn into clothing linings, or hidden within the folds of market baskets.

Disguises played an important role. Messengers sometimes dressed as fishmongers, milkmaids, or even beggars to pass unseen through British checkpoints. A servant girl might leave a Loyalist home carrying laundry; inside her apron, a note described a sudden gathering of officers at Boston Common. Some men feigned drunkenness at taverns to eavesdrop on soldiers boasting about upcoming operations. These small acts of deception proved invaluable, allowing information to flow out of the city even when Redcoat patrols tightened their hold.

Critical moments hinged on the success of these covert efforts. The night before the British march to Lexington and Concord, Warren's network detected unusual activity near Boston's barracks and wharves—troops mustering quietly, supplies being loaded without fanfare, officers conferring behind closed doors. One informant overheard enough to understand that a major expedition was imminent. He relayed this to Warren in hurried whispers as dusk fell. Warren then dispatched Paul Revere and William Dawes with precise warnings about the British objectives and likely routes—a move that proved decisive, giving the colonial militias precious hours to prepare.

The alarm system functioned because these informants worked tirelessly and selflessly. They had no guarantee of safety and little chance for public recognition. Some were nearly caught as they slipped messages to Patriot leaders; others faced direct threats from Loyalists or British authorities who suspected their loyalties. One anonymous shop assistant endured a midnight search of her employer's house after a rumor spread about hidden Patriot correspondence—she hid her note behind a loose brick in the hearth, trembling as soldiers overturned furniture around her. Another man, caught lingering near a British encampment with a sketch of troop positions folded in his pocket, endured hours of interrogation before he convinced his captors he was merely lost.

Personal sacrifice defined the life of every spy and messenger in Warren's network. Some lost jobs after Loyalist employers grew suspicious; several found themselves ostracized by neighbors who feared British retaliation. Others lived with constant anxiety for their families' safety, knowing that discovery would mean not just arrest but possible violence or exile. Despite these dangers, they persisted—motivated by the conviction that their efforts could prevent disaster and preserve liberty.

The effectiveness of Warren's intelligence system lay in its adaptability and reach. Messages passed quickly across class lines and through unexpected channels; a stable boy might overhear an officer's careless remark and pass it on through an elderly matron who visited the market each morning. Sometimes information arrived piecemeal—a whispered warning here, a coded note there—but Warren and his core group pieced together these fragments with remarkable accuracy.

Historians have since uncovered anonymous writings and secondhand accounts describing midnight meetings and coded signals exchanged under watchful British eyes. These sources reveal both the ingenuity and the peril faced by Boston's hidden patriots. Even without names attached to every act of courage, their contributions remain evident: without their vigilance and willingness to risk all for a cause greater than themselves, the alarm raised on April 18 might have come too late—or not at all.

The story of Boston's colonial spies is not just one of clever tactics but also of daily courage—a reminder that revolutions depend on those willing to watch quietly, act quickly, and often remain forever unnamed. Their legacy lingers in every account of those tense hours before dawn broke over Lexington Green, when the fate of two nations teetered on what was whispered in back rooms and carried swiftly out into the night.

The Towns Awaken – Muster Drums and Family Goodbyes

Before dawn, the towns of Lexington, Concord, and nearby villages pulsed with unfamiliar urgency. The first hint was often a drumbeat, steady and insistent, rolling through the night air. Church bells pealed with frantic energy, their tolling echoing against wood-planked homes and empty lanes. Windows flickered as candles flared. Doors flew open. Footsteps hurried down narrow paths, and the sound of men's voices—quick, rough, and anxious—filled the lanes. In many homes, the day's rhythm shattered as fathers roused sons from sleep, mothers whispered urgent instructions, and children blinked in confusion. The ordinary quiet of nighttime dissolved into a rush of preparation; every family understood that something irreversible had begun.

Inside small kitchens and crowded parlors, families moved with practiced efficiency. Men reached for powder horns and muskets, hands shaking as they checked supplies. Some scribbled quick notes—short goodbyes or hurried instructions for those staying behind. Letters and oral traditions from these towns recall parting words laced with fear and hope. One Lexington wife remembered her husband's last embrace, his voice steady but his eyes wet, telling her to keep the children safe if he did not return. A Concord mother later described blessing her teenage son at the doorstep, pressing a crust of bread into his hand while fighting to hold back tears.

Women played vital roles in these hours. They loaded cartridges, measured powder, and filled shot pouches as briskly as any militiaman. Bread baked overnight was wrapped in linen and packed into haversacks. Some women boiled water or steeped herbs for tea, knowing their husbands might march for hours without rest. Livestock needed tending—cows milked, chickens fed—chores done quickly now that men would not be home by sunrise. In several homes, mothers soothed frightened children and reminded them to care for younger siblings. Elders, too old for the ranks but unwilling to stand idle, offered advice on repairing gun flints or mending uniforms. Some walked to neighbors' houses to help with preparations or to care for infants left behind.

The emotional charge in each home was unmistakable. Fear lingered close; courage was not the absence of dread but the decision to act despite it. Prayers rose from many households—some silent, others led aloud by trembling voices gathered around kitchen tables or fireplaces. Meetinghouses became sanctuaries where neighbors gathered for blessing and reassurance. Clergy stood at the front doors or along the green, offering words of comfort and faith to men heading into danger. In Lexington, Reverend Jonas Clarke reportedly reminded the militia that they stood not just for themselves but for all who valued liberty and justice.

Outside, the night air vibrated with nervous anticipation. Some men lingered at their thresholds, reluctant to leave loved ones behind. Others strode quickly toward the green or common, joining clusters of friends and neighbors who looked equally uncertain but fiercely determined. The muster was not a parade; it was a summoning of ordinary people—farmers, blacksmiths, cobblers—called by necessity into roles they never sought but could not refuse.

The atmosphere in each town was charged with a mixture of resolve and anxiety. No one knew exactly what would come next. Would the British regulars pass through quietly, or would blood be spilled on familiar ground? As men assembled in the half-darkness, their faces revealed a spectrum of emotion: worry for those at home, pride in standing together, fear of the unknown.

As dawn approached, these communities faced their fate not as passive witnesses but as active participants in history. The decisions made during these dark hours set the stage for everything that followed—the first shots on Lexington Green, the resistance at Concord's North Bridge, and the long struggle for independence that would reshape a continent.

In these moments before sunrise, ordinary families became part of something extraordinary. The courage shown in kitchens and on commons echoed far beyond Massachusetts. Each farewell carried hope that tomorrow would bring reunion rather than mourning. Each prayer uttered in fear or faith gave strength to those facing the march ahead.

This night of alarms did not just awaken towns—it awakened a people. The next chapter will bring you onto Lexington Green itself, where tension finally snaps and history changes course forever.

Chapter 3: April 19th, 1775 The Road to Lexington

2:00–4:00 a.m. – The British Column Crosses the Charles

In the pre-dawn hours, Boston's streets buzzed with anticipation. If you had been near Boston Common, you'd have seen shadows—British soldiers moving quietly and purposefully, boots muffled on damp ground. Officers whispered urgent orders as small groups gathered by the water, shouldering full equipment in near silence. The long whaleboats waited in the moonlight, and men loaded them carefully, avoiding any splash or clatter. Even the horses led among the men were subdued, sensing the tension. The city seemed held in suspense, every movement cautious, and every glance wary in case Patriot eyes were watching.

General Gage's strategy relied on speed and secrecy, hoping to reach his objectives before word could spread. Officers, many not much older than their men, nervously checked their watches and reviewed handwritten orders. The soldiers were drawn from elite regiments—grenadiers and light infantry of the 23rd Royal Welch Fusiliers, the 4th Regiment of Foot, and others—selected for their discipline. Yet, even among veterans, nerves were exposed. Hushed exchanges ranged from bravado about "country rebels" to concern or confusion about their true mission. Many had never seen live battle; for some, this was their first experience outside Britain.

Crossing the Charles River was a challenge in itself. The wide water, chilled and foggy under fading night, heightened the sense of risk. Oarsmen rowed with quiet, synchronized strokes, careful to avoid drawing attention. Soldiers crammed shoulder to shoulder in each boat, clutching muskets and kit, aware that even a breath might break the hush. "The silence was a thing alive," recalled one officer, "I thought I could hear my heart above the splash of our oars." The cold bit through coats, making many shiver uncontrollably.

Landing in Cambridge was no easier. Boats grounded on muddy shores at Lechmere Point and Phipps Farm—chosen for their access to key roads and distance from Patriot surveillance. Officers were first ashore, steadying the crafts so men, equipment, and horses could be quickly moved onto land. Supplies—powder, ammunition, rations—were hastily, silently offloaded and passed hand to hand. Soon, soldiers fell into line, officers checking weapons and consulting shielded lanterns for readiness. Maps were unfurled, and rough plans for the march to Lexington and Concord were traced in the flickering light, with officers aware that every lost minute risked warning the countryside.

Despite fears, British discipline prevailed. Sergeants issued commands in hushed tones; lieutenants used covered lanterns to check lists and read faces for fatigue or anxiety. Officers traced routes toward their targets and set the pace for the march, knowing that every delay helped the Patriots.

For young soldiers, many barely out of their teens, the night was overwhelming. Letters written soon after reveal their anxiety and pride in being part of such a momentous mission. A private from the 23rd Royal Welch Fusiliers wrote home: "the night was colder than I imagined, my hands numb before we landed... I could not shake the feeling we marched into something larger than any drill." Another noted in his diary how even sleeping Cambridge "seemed unfriendly; I watched for movement at every window." These accounts remind us that beneath the British uniforms were young men, anxious, eager, and uncertain what the day might bring.

For the soldiers of April 19, 1775, each detail mattered— the muddy ground beneath their boots, a whispered order from an officer, and the growing weight of musket and pack as dawn edged across the sky.

The Long Road to Lexington – Terrain, Weather, and Hidden Dangers

As the British column set off from Cambridge, the landscape soon dictated the pace and mood of the march. Fields gave way to patches of thick woods, tangled with undergrowth still glistening from a cold April dew. The road itself wound and narrowed, sometimes little more than a rutted lane bordered by ancient stone walls or split-rail fences. In places, swampy ground pressed close on either side, forcing soldiers into single file where footing grew soft and treacherous. Farmhouses appeared at intervals, their windows dark but never quite empty—every shutter a potential spyhole, every barn a question mark. The countryside in these hours felt close and watchful, the usual peace of farmland replaced by a sense of scrutiny.

The dampness hung heavy. Clouds drifted low, and the air carried a raw edge that seeped through uniforms and numbed fingers. The darkness before dawn made every step uncertain. Lanterns were strictly forbidden by officers demanding perfect stealth, so men stumbled over rocks and roots or splashed through hidden puddles. Muskets grew slick in clammy hands. The British regulars trudged forward in near silence, boots muffled by soft earth, breaths clouding as they passed through hollows and over ridges. The weather shaped more than discomfort; it masked the troops' approach from distant eyes but also threatened to sap their resolve before any shot was fired.

For many soldiers, the march became a test of nerves as much as body. The threat of ambush lingered with every step. Colonists had a reputation for sharp eyes and quick action; each bend in the road presented the possibility of musket fire from behind a stone wall or a sudden volley from an orchard's shadow. Some men thought they saw movement among the trees—a hat vanishing behind a fence post, a glint of metal that might be a musket barrel or simply morning dew catching the first hint of light. These "false alarms" rippled down the ranks, making even seasoned officers tense. Once, near a stand of maples, a startled owl burst from its roost and set off dozens of hearts pounding. Others reported hearing distant bells or dogs barking—a sign that their presence was already known and the countryside was stirring to life.

The geography itself worked against speed and cohesion. Menotomy—now called Arlington—sat astride the main road, a strategic village where several lanes converged. Passing through Menotomy meant navigating not only its narrow main street but also crossing creeks that could slow wagons or scatter formations. At every crossroads, British officers felt exposed, knowing that even a brief halt gave Patriot watchers time to count numbers or estimate their direction. Bridges—simple wooden spans over muddy brooks—became choke points where columns bunched up, and discipline frayed. A single overturned cart could block progress for minutes that felt like hours.

Beyond Menotomy, the land opened into stretches of open farmland dotted with stone outcroppings and thickets of brush. These fields looked peaceful but offered perfect cover for any determined group of militia. The column's flanks were vulnerable whenever fences or woods edged too close to the road. Officers posted extra sentries at these spots, their eyes scanning furrows and hayricks for signs of movement.

The psychological strain mounted as the distance to Lexington shrank. Every mile added to the fatigue born not just from cold and hunger but from expectation—every unexpected sound or flicker in the dark might signal the beginning of violence. The British had received orders to avoid unnecessary alarm, but discipline sometimes faltered when nerves ran high. Men whispered rumors: some claimed they had seen armed farmers at crossroads; others reported signal lanterns swinging in distant barns—a message for Patriot forces to gather ahead.

Despite these fears, no real attack came during this march. Yet each moment without conflict did nothing to ease anxiety; instead, it heightened the sense that danger might erupt at any second. By the time the first gray light crept over the fields near Lexington, both officers and men were exhausted but alert—acutely aware they had crossed into territory where every hedge might hide an enemy and every quiet village could become a battleground.

The route's geography had done its work: slowing progress, scattering attention, feeding suspicion, and setting the conditions for what would unfold next on Lexington Green.

Encounters in the Night – Loyalist Guides and Colonial Scouts

British officers knew the countryside beyond Cambridge was a puzzle of twisting lanes, uneven tracks, and hidden farmsteads. Many had marched in foreign lands, but Massachusetts presented its own challenge—familiar to locals, a labyrinth for outsiders. To navigate these roads, the British command relied on Loyalist guides. These men, openly supporting the Crown or quietly loyal, offered both information and direction. Some did so for reward or protection; others out of conviction or fear of retribution from their Patriot neighbors. Daniel Murray, a known Loyalist from the area, stands as a clear example. He helped the British maneuver through the dark, pointing out less-traveled byways and warning of places where Patriot sentiment ran high. Officers depended on men like Murray to avoid dead ends or dangerous crossroads. The trust placed in these guides was immense, and each step taken depended on their loyalty holding firm.

Yet, the British column was not alone on the roads. Patriots had their own network—scouts, spies, and informants who blended with the landscape. If you imagine yourself crouched behind a tumbled stone wall or pressed low among the apple trees, you understand how these men worked: eyes sharp for movement, ears tuned to the distant thud of marching boots. Colonial scouts moved in small groups or alone, shadowing the redcoats at a distance. Some counted regimental colors or estimated troop numbers in whispered exchanges before slipping away to carry news back to waiting militia. The tension was thick; every snapped branch or shifting shadow could mean discovery. These men risked capture or worse but persisted, knowing their reports could shape the coming fight.

Encounters between these opposing watchers were inevitable in such close quarters. On one stretch near Menotomy, a Patriot scout stumbled upon a British patrol moving ahead of the main column. Breath held, he flattened into the roadside ditch as soldiers passed within arm's reach, muskets ready. In another instance, a Loyalist guide pointed out what he thought was an abandoned barn—only for a colonial observer to bolt from its shadows and vanish into the woods before pursuit could be mounted. There were moments when British troops captured wandering locals on suspicion of spying. A young farmhand named Isaac Hall was stopped and questioned under threat, but managed to convince his captors he was simply heading home from a late errand. Sometimes these were true; often, they were not.

Communication among colonial scouts relied on code words and signals. A lantern flashed three times from an attic window meant "enemy advancing," while a rooster's crow at the wrong hour signaled movement on the road. Notes scribbled quickly with charcoal on scraps of paper passed from hand to hand in barns, taverns, and churchyards—each message relaying British numbers, direction, or unusual behavior. Local boys sometimes acted as runners, darting across fields with news for their fathers or neighbors already mustered at prearranged points.

Despite all this effort, information did not always flow smoothly. There were lapses—moments when news arrived too late or was garbled by rumor. A false report that British troops had turned back sent one group of militia home just as another was preparing to move out. At times, two scouts brought conflicting stories about enemy strength or position, leaving leaders like Captain John Parker in Lexington with hard choices and little clarity. Still, enough messages reached their targets to give towns like Concord precious time to ready defenses and hide stores of powder.

The flow of intelligence shaped every decision that morning. In Lexington, word from scouts prompted Parker to call his men together before dawn, urging caution but also readiness. In Concord, a flurry of messages brought warnings so detailed that town leaders began moving supplies before the first redcoats reached the outskirts. When communication worked well, it allowed Patriots to anticipate British moves and organize effective resistance; when it failed, it left gaps that could mean disaster.

On the British side, reliance on Loyalist guides sometimes led to confusion as well. Not all guides knew every lane or hidden footpath; some underestimated local resistance or failed to spot warning signals flashed from farmhouse windows. Misinformation could send columns down muddy detours or through hamlets already emptied by alarm riders. The burden fell on officers to weigh local advice against military instinct—a balance rarely easy in unfamiliar terrain where every misstep might be fatal.

Both sides learned quickly that knowledge was power—often more decisive than guns or numbers at this stage of conflict. The battle for information played out in the silent fields and shadowed lanes long before any musket fired on Lexington Green. Each report carried weight; each guide's word could tip the scales between surprise and disaster for hundreds waiting in darkness just ahead.

Side Stories – Women, Children, and the Alarm at Home

When the first warnings rattled the countryside, homes in Lexington, Concord, and scattered hamlets stirred in confusion and dread. Family routines fractured as doors flew open and hurried voices filled the chill night. Mothers snapped awake at the urgent pounding from neighbors or the frantic tolling of the meetinghouse bell. Children, startled from dreams, clung to their bedcovers or rushed to windows, eyes wide as their fathers yanked muskets from above the hearth or laced boots by candlelight. The darkness outside pressed close, making every sound seem sharper and more dangerous.

Inside kitchens, women's hands moved fast. Diaries tell how Mary Munroe in Lexington swept valuables—silver spoons, family papers—into flour sacks, then stashed them under loose floorboards or behind stone walls. Some women hid their best pewter or treasured books in haylofts, fearing British soldiers might plunder anything left in sight. Others boiled water for tea or baked loaves of bread, knowing men would need food before facing whatever came at dawn. The smell of fresh bread mingled with gun oil and sweat, a strange comfort in a night of uncertainty.

These mothers, wives, and sisters did more than prepare supplies. They became anchors for their families, steadying trembling hands and offering quiet words of courage. Once husbands and sons hurried out into the darkness, women gathered in clusters—sometimes in a neighbor's parlor, sometimes in the shadowed pews of the church. There, they whispered prayers for safety and strength. Some read from battered Bibles, while others simply stared into the flicker of candles, lips moving in silent petition. Their fear was real, but so was their resolve. In Concord, Abigail Brooks wrote to her cousin that she had "watched the windows for any sign of return and joined hands with Mrs. Barrett, praying our men would have wisdom and God's protection." Each house became a small fortress of hope and anxiety.

The youngest members of these households struggled to understand the upheaval all around them. One boy later recalled crouching at his mother's skirts as neighbors rushed past their door, boots thudding on packed earth. Another remembered hiding under a table, his ears full of shouted names and orders he could not comprehend. Fear mixed with fascination—the sight of men mustering on the green or the sudden arrival of a mounted messenger became memories that never faded. A girl in Lincoln described peeking out to see her brother, barely older than herself, struggling to keep up with the older men as they marched away.

Yet children did not only witness history; sometimes they took part. Nine-year-old Jonathan Harrington carried a pitcher of water to his grandfather outside Buckman Tavern before sunrise, too young to fight but determined to help. In some families, older children helped their mothers melt bits of lead for musket balls or tore up old linen for bandages. The crisis brought out courage in small gestures—a whispered comfort to a frightened sibling, a steady hand holding a lantern by the door as fathers left.

For all these families, waiting became its own ordeal. With men gone and the threat of violence hanging over every village, women traded rumors and fragments of news with nervous urgency. One story might claim the British had turned back; another insisted gunfire had already begun on the green. Candles burned low as wives paced floorboards or stared out blackened windows for any sign—a distant shot, a running figure on the road—that would bring news of loved ones. In Concord, a circle of mothers huddled near Wright's Tavern when a young rider galloped by with a shout that "the Regulars have reached Lexington." The women clutched each other's arms and prayed harder.

The uncertainty gnawed at every household. Anxiety moved through walls as surely as the wind outside. Some women gathered children behind locked doors, listening for every footstep or muffled shout from the street. Others stayed on their porches, scanning the road for returning militia or for news brought by breathless boys sent home as messengers. Many found themselves comforting not only their own families but anxious neighbors—offering bread, shelter, or simply a steady presence.

These scenes played out across Massachusetts that April morning—at once ordinary and extraordinary. Fear, hope, and determination filled the hours before dawn. The courage shown by women and children shaped how families endured crisis and how communities found the resilience to face whatever would come with sunrise.

Lexington Green at Dawn – Captain Parker's Dilemma

As first light crept into the sky, Lexington Green stretched out in a gentle triangle at the village center. The grass was damp, the air heavy with an April chill that seeped into boots and bones. All around, the pale blue of dawn met the dark silhouettes of houses—Buckman Tavern to the east, the meetinghouse to the west, Reverend Clarke's parsonage nearby. A few leafless elms reached upward, their branches stark against the growing light. The main road came from Boston and angled sharply across the green, with smaller paths radiating outward to Concord and Woburn. From every direction, you'd see clusters of men moving toward the green, their shapes blurred by mist, some on foot, a handful leading horses. The field was open, but the buildings and walls offered points to watch or shelter, and every door seemed to hold a face peering out into the uncertain morning.

Captain John Parker stood at the center of it all. He was a man in his mid-forties, his health worn by tuberculosis, but his presence steady. No one envied his burden that morning. He had heard alarms for hours—a patchwork of news: British regulars marching from Boston, unknown numbers, unclear intentions. Some whispers claimed the soldiers would seize powder; others warned of arrests. Parker's mind raced, caught between duty and doubt. He recalled his own service in earlier wars and weighed each option: Should he stand firm and risk his men's lives? Should he disperse and risk being caught off guard? His famous words—"Stand your ground; don't fire unless fired upon, but if they mean to have a war, let it begin here"—were not empty bravado. They came from deep uncertainty, from responsibility for neighbors who had never faced professional soldiers before.

The news Parker received was confusing and sometimes contradictory. Messengers came breathless, reporting hundreds—perhaps a thousand—redcoats on the march. Others said the British might only want a show of force. Some officers urged caution, wanting to avoid needless bloodshed; others argued for standing together so Lexington would not appear weak or divided. Townsmen brought their own anxieties—fathers of young boys urging restraint, veterans remembering past violence, urging resolve. Every new arrival with "the latest" brought another layer of worry or hope. Some pointed to the thickening line of militia as proof they could deter the enemy; others feared they were hopelessly outnumbered and exposed.

The state of the militia reflected this tension. Men gathered in uneven lines: some clutching old muskets handed down from fathers or uncles, others arriving half-dressed, powder horns swinging at their sides. There were farmers with dirt still under their nails, shopkeepers who had left their ledgers open on counters, apprentices barely old enough for whiskers. Stalwart friends like Jonas Parker—older but fiercely determined—stood shoulder to shoulder with their sons and nephews. Teenage boys mixed nervously among their elders, eager but pale, their hats too large and coats too thin for the morning cold. Some men had cartridges neatly packed and muskets primed; others fumbled with damp powder as their eyes darted between Captain Parker and the distant road.

Eyewitnesses later wrote about these moments—some with pride, others with trembling honesty. One militiaman remembered his hands shaking so badly he could hardly fit flint into the lock of his musket. Another described how his father clapped him on the shoulder and whispered, "You mind Captain Parker." Several spoke simply of waiting: "We stood there not knowing what would come next." The air was thick with unspoken questions. Some wanted to return home; others feared shame if they left their spot in line. A few men prayed quietly under their breath; others stared straight ahead at nothing, jaw set.

Militiamen continued to arrive as dawn brightened—their numbers never large but enough to give Parker pause before making any decision. The line wavered and shifted as men took places according to age or family ties. In one corner of the green, a cluster of older men stood apart, watching for British uniforms on the horizon. Near Buckman Tavern, several younger boys tried to look braver than they felt as they copied their fathers' stances.

The tension rose with every moment that passed without clarity. No one knew if they would face a peaceful negotiation or sudden violence. Parker wrestled with responsibility—not only for tactics but for lives he valued as neighbors and kin. He was forced to act on imperfect information and conflicting counsel, trusting instinct and honor over certainty. The sun edged higher as mist began to burn away, revealing more faces gathering along the green's edge—each waiting for a signal from their captain or a sign from the approaching British column that would decide what kind of history Lexington would write that day.

The Gathering of Militiamen – Who Answered the Call?

As the first blue streaks of morning crept over Lexington, clusters of men converged on the green from every direction. Muster rolls and town records paint a vivid portrait of these early responders. Lexington's own militia stood at the center—neighbors whose names echoed in town meetings and church ledgers: Jonas Parker, Isaac Muzzy, Robert Munroe, and Prince Estabrook, among others. From nearby communities, reinforcements trickled in. Woburn's men arrived in small groups, boots caked in spring mud, faces drawn tight with worry and resolve. Men from Lincoln, Bedford, and Menotomy were not far behind, some traveling all night after hearing the alarm. Each arrival brought new energy and fresh uncertainty.

Within the ranks, every walk of life found a place. The faces on the green reflected the region's social fabric—farmers with rough hands and sunburned forearms, blacksmiths whose arms bore the memory of hammers, cobblers who left their benches and tools behind in haste.

There were barrel makers, schoolteachers, millers, and apprentices barely grown. Some men wore their Sunday best; others came in hunting frocks, whatever was closest at hand. The ages varied widely. Jonas Parker, gray-haired and stoic, stood firm despite bad joints and years of hard labor.

He was joined by his son and cousins—a family line resolved to stand together no matter the outcome. Nearby stood Prince Estabrook, a black freeman enslaved by the Estabrook family, but here counted as an equal in defense of his town. At about thirty-five years old, Prince had seen hardship but faced this morning's uncertainty with the same steadiness as any other man in line. His presence revealed how the call to arms cut across boundaries of status and birth.

Next to him stood young William Tidd, just coming of age, his first battle looming before he'd finished learning a trade. Several teenage boys pressed close to fathers or uncles for guidance and courage.

Family bonds ran deep through the crowd. Brothers stood shoulder to shoulder; fathers kept an eye on sons who tried to hide their nerves behind bravado. Neighbors nodded silent greetings—the kind you exchange when words feel heavy or inadequate. For many families, several male relatives mustered together, knowing the risk but trusting in each other's strength. The line on Lexington Green was not only a military formation but an assembly of kin and community.

Organizing these men required both discipline and improvisation. Officers moved among the ranks, calling names from hastily scribbled lists. Drummers like young William Diamond beat a steady rhythm on taut calfskin heads, signaling instructions above the low hum of anxious talk. Messengers darted between groups with updates—

how many men had arrived, which direction British troops might be coming from, whether ammunition was running low, or more powder was needed from nearby houses. Captain Parker and his lieutenants worked to position each unit—some facing the main road from Boston, others angled toward side lanes where surprise might come. Orders passed quietly: "Hold your fire," "Stand steady," "Wait for command." The green became a living diagram of hope and preparation.

The atmosphere crackled with anticipation. Every sound seemed magnified: the distant crow of a rooster, boots scraping on frozen grass, the occasional cough muffled behind a sleeve. Men shifted from foot to foot to keep warm; breath hung in clouds that vanished as quickly as nerves would allow. Some gripped muskets so tightly their knuckles whitened; others fingered powder horns or checked flints for the third or fourth time. Conversation dwindled to whispers as the moment approached.

Eyewitnesses recalled the tension that settled just before sunrise, describing it as a hush "before the thunder." Jonas Parker's jaw clenched as he looked down the road—his family's future uncertain with every tick of the clock. Prince Estabrook glanced once at his neighbors before fixing his gaze on the tree line ahead. William Tidd admitted years later that he felt both proud to stand with his elders and terrified by what might follow. For all present, time seemed to slow as they waited for history to catch up with them.

As more militiamen took their places and dawn broke fully over Lexington Green, the weight of what was coming pressed on every heart. These not professional soldiers—they were fathers, sons, craftsmen, laborers—ordinary people joined by duty and circumstance.

With sunrise came clarity: this was no drill nor rumor but a moment that demanded resolve beyond fear or doubt. Each man assembled there carried not only a musket but the hopes of family and town. They waited together in silence as red coats appeared on the horizon—ready or not—for whatever history would demand next.

When you think about who answered the call that morning, remember it was not only their weapons but their character that shaped what happened next. Communities found strength in unity; families faced danger side by side; individuals stepped forward so that freedom could take its first uncertain steps on American soil.

The chapter closes here, with neighbors gathered on Lexington Green—poised for confrontation under a sky quickly brightening with promise and peril. Ahead lies the clash itself: shots fired, lives changed, legends born out of ordinary courage and extraordinary consequence.

—

Chapter 4: Shots on Lexington Green The World Changes in Minutes

5:30–5:45 a.m. – British Advance Guard Arrives

At first, the dawn on Lexington Green might have seemed like any other, the air just cold. But those present felt the ground vibrate as Major John Pitcairn's advance guard emerged on Boston Road. The British troops—disciplined, orderly, and dressed in immaculate red uniforms—advanced in perfect formation, their bayonets reflecting the rising sun. The sight made a powerful impression: the overwhelming force and discipline of the British army was on full display, mesmerizing and frightening the locals.

A map of the green at that hour reveals British light infantry forming a broad line from the east, blocking the road. Pitcairn's troops maneuvered with crisp commands, closing ranks as they advanced. The Lexington militia stood loosely on the northern edge. Landmarks surrounded them: Buckman Tavern to the northwest, the meetinghouse at the south corner, and homes with candlelit windows. Townspeople watched quietly—children pressed to glass, women huddled in shawls, and men hovering behind stone walls and fences, unsure whether to join the fight or remain out of sight.

For the British, months of drilling in Boston had forged discipline, but as they stepped onto the green, the sight of armed locals gave even experienced soldiers pause. Morning light accentuated every detail—the tricolor cockades, polished brass, rhythmic marching. The militiamen, awed and anxious, clutched their muskets tightly. William Diamond, the young Lexington drummer, later remembered how "the ground seemed to tremble" as the redcoats advanced and how a "coldness in my chest I could not shake" lingered. This was a real confrontation—not just practice.

Major Pitcairn projected command, riding forward and calling out, "Disperse, ye villains! Lay down your arms!" His tone left no room for doubt. Other officers echoed his order, urging the colonists to scatter and avoid harm. Some accounts say Pitcairn tried to reassure the militia, insisting they would face no danger if they left. But the tension was unmistakable. On the green, militiamen looked to one another or to Captain Parker for cues. Some shifted nervously; others held their ground.

The militia's discipline showed cracks under immense pressure. A few moved back, while others stayed rooted. From nearby homes, witnesses could hear "a great confusion of voices" as British officers repeated their warnings and the militiamen murmured uncertainties. For a long moment, no one made the first move; time seemed to stand still as both sides balanced on the edge of disaster.

The British regulars maintained their formation, bayonets angled forward, sending a clear message of intent. The red-coated line, muskets ready, contrasted sharply with the scattered, nervous militia—a mix of young and old, often family members side by side. It was a striking scene: British order facing American resolve, empire demanding obedience against local determination.

This confrontation was more than just a military standoff; it was a meeting of worlds, with an empire seeking obedience from a community defending its principles. The silence was charged, commands ringing out while both sides hesitated. William Diamond never forgot the fear: "I heard one officer shout again for us to go home… but we did not know what to do." Pitcairn, too, would later insist he wanted to avoid violence—ordering his men not to fire unless provoked.

But in reality, nobody could control what was about to happen. As officers' orders grew urgent and the militia wavered, each second heightened the tension. The townspeople—families and neighbors—**"Stand Your Ground" – Captain Parker's Commands**

The sun had barely lifted above the horizon when Captain John Parker, at the center of Lexington Green, made his stand. He was not a man who sought glory or conflict. Years of illness and war had worn his body, but his mind remained sharp. He watched his neighbors—some still young, others seasoned—forming a ragged line across the green. Their breaths steamed in the cold air, hands gripping muskets, eyes flickering between Parker and the advance of Pitcairn's redcoats. The tension was thick enough to taste.

Parker's order cut through the morning hush: "Stand your ground. Don't fire unless fired upon, but if they mean to have a war, let it begin here." The phrase, now carved in stone and memory, reflected more than bravado. Parker knew his men faced overwhelming odds. He could see the British numbers, their discipline, their bayonets glinting in the growing light. Yet he would not have his neighbors scatter in panic, nor would he let them become the aggressors. That moment called for resolve—quiet courage, not reckless action. His words echoed across the green, reaching every ear, from Jonas Parker at the front rank to Ebenezer Munroe and others steadying their nerves further back.

Eyewitnesses described the weight in Parker's voice. Jonas Parker, a relative of the captain, later recalled how each man felt loyalty not only to cause but to kin. Ebenezer Munroe remembered a hush broken only by whispers—"Hold your fire"—and the soft shuffle of boots settling into place. Several men later testified that Parker commanded restraint above all: "No man to discharge his piece unless first fired upon." The ambiguity gnawed at every mind. What if a musket went off by mistake? What if someone misunderstood? Each second stretched into eternity, anxiety building as redcoats drew closer.

The militia's discipline held against instinctive fear. Some men clenched their muskets so tightly that their knuckles whitened. Others glanced sideways at friends or fathers beside them, searching for reassurance or silent agreement. A few exchanged words under their breath—brief prayers, last-minute advice about aiming true, or warnings not to run unless ordered. Their line was not perfect; bodies shifted, some edging forward, others drifting back unconsciously toward Buckman Tavern. Yet most stood firm, feet planted on muddy grass, faces set with determination and uncertainty.

Physical spacing on the green mattered deeply in those minutes. The Lexington militia formed a line roughly parallel to the meetinghouse and facing east toward Boston Road. Buckman Tavern anchored their left flank; the meetinghouse stood just behind their right. Between them and the British stretched open space—estimates put it at about seventy yards at first, though some witnesses believed it was less by the time orders were exchanged. This gap became a living thing: too far for easy conversation, close enough for each side to see faces and read intent. It was wide enough that a single voice might not reach all ears, but narrow enough for any sudden move to trigger disaster.

Testimonies from those present reveal how critical this formation was. Jonas Parker knelt where the line bent toward the tavern—he would not yield ground as long as he breathed. Other men farther down the row watched both the British advance and their own captain with equal intensity. Some officers walked behind the ranks, reinforcing Parker's command that no one fire without orders. The men closest to Boston Road felt exposed but trusted Parker's judgment more than their own nerves.

Despite outward composure, anxiety ran deep among the militia. Each heartbeat seemed to thunder in their chests as they waited. Some shifted weight from foot to foot; a few looked backward to see if retreat was possible if things went wrong. Whispered conversations ebbed and flowed:

"Should we step back?" "Wait for Parker." "They're loading." "Hold fast." The discipline required in that moment was immense—not just military but personal, as each man struggled with fear and pride.

The militia knew they were being watched not just by British eyes but by neighbors' families gathered at windows or peering from behind fences. The presence of sisters, wives, and children made every decision heavier. No one wanted to be remembered as a coward, nor as someone who started a war with an impulsive shot. So they held their line, watching British bayonets draw ever closer.

From later depositions and letters collected by Massachusetts authorities, we know that distances shrank rapidly as the British pressed forward (APA list: 1; 6). Some colonists claimed the regulars closed within "a few rods"— less than thirty yards—before anything happened. Even then, Parker's order remained clear in memory: hold your ground until fired upon.

The discipline of these men—untested in open battle—held as tightly as any drilled regiment might hope for under such strain. When fate finally broke loose on Lexington Green, it was not because these farmers failed their captain or lost command of themselves, but because events outran every order and intention that had held so briefly but so bravely at Parker's word.

Who Fired the First Shot? – Testimonies, Contradictions, and Evidence

The question of who fired the first shot at Lexington is as stubborn as the morning mist that clung to the green that day. If you read the accounts left behind, you find yourself caught in a maze of words—each testimony a window into the chaos, but no single voice holding all the truth. Captain John Parker, in his sworn deposition, declared with certainty that his men stood fast and did not fire until fired upon. He wrote that he ordered restraint, insisting, "I immediately ordered our Militia to disperse, and not to fire." Parker's men repeated this same claim. Ebenezer Munroe testified, "I never heard any orders given to fire, nor did I see any person fire before the regulars fired upon us." These words, collected by the Massachusetts Provincial Congress soon after the event, form one side of the story—a chorus of restraint and self-control.

British accounts stand in sharp contrast. Major John Pitcairn reported that he rode forward to urge the militia to lay down arms and go home. In his statement, Pitcairn argued that the colonists fired first from behind a stone wall or some distant cover. Some British soldiers echoed his view, describing how a shot seemed to come from behind a hedge or from an "unknown" direction. One private claimed he saw "a flash in the pan" from the colonial side before any redcoat fired. To British officers, this volley became proof of colonial aggression; they insisted their men only returned fire after being attacked.

Both sides presented their versions with passionate conviction, but contradictions run through every account. Colonial militiamen swore they never fired first, while British officers denied any intention of opening fire without cause. Yet some details remain consistent: almost all agree that an order to disperse was given, and that confusion reigned in those tense seconds. Theories have flourished over the centuries—a musket discharging by accident, a nervous finger on a flintlock trigger, or even a shot from a bystander or distant house. Some suggest a colonial gun went off as its owner fled, or that a British musket discharged as soldiers jostled into line. Each theory has its supporters, but none can be proven beyond doubt.

Motivations for shaping these stories are not hard to find. The colonial depositions were collected by Patriot leaders determined to build support for their cause; they had every reason to emphasize restraint and innocence. The British officers, facing scrutiny from their superiors and the government at home, needed to justify their actions and avoid blame for starting a war. Both groups shaped their memories under pressure, with reputations and perhaps lives at stake.

Confusion clouded every perception on Lexington Green. The smoke from black powder muskets quickly drifted across the field, making it hard to see who fired and when. The acoustics of the open space and nearby buildings caused echoes—one shot might sound like several, shouts layered upon each other until all clarity vanished. Witnesses described hearing voices, then a single report, then more shots in chaotic succession. Some men recalled the first sound as distant or behind them; others swore it came from directly ahead.

The chaos of overlapping commands further muddied memory. Both Parker and Pitcairn were shouting orders— some men remember hearing "Lay down your arms!" while others recall "Don't fire!" The crash of muskets, combined with yells from both sides and the screams of frightened townspeople, made it almost impossible for anyone to know what happened in those first seconds. Panic spread as quickly as smoke; once one musket fired, others followed almost instantly.

Myth-Busting Panel: "The Shot Heard 'Round the World" – Legend and Analysis

The phrase "the shot heard 'round the world" has captured imaginations for generations, but it is more poetry than fact. No single musket shot can be traced to any one man on Lexington Green. Forensic reconstructions—using modern sound analysis and battlefield archaeology—have not settled the matter either. Black powder muskets do not leave shell casings or precise ballistic evidence; spent balls and shattered ramrods found near the green only show how fierce the volley became after firing began. No eyewitness could untangle the exact sequence in those fractured seconds.

Historians agree on this much: uncertainty is built into the fabric of Lexington's story. What we know is shaped by memory under stress, by political needs on both sides, and by the simple fact that chaos makes truth slippery. The legend of a single moment—the "shot heard 'round the world"—has power because it marks a turning point in history, but the reality is far messier and more human than myth allows.

So when you stand on Lexington Green today or read these testimonies yourself, remember that answers are always tangled with doubt. What happened there is not just a question for scholars; it is a reminder that history's most important moments—those that change lives and nations—are often shrouded in confusion, contradiction, and voices raised above the roar of musket fire (APA list: 1; 6; 3; 4).

The Chaos of the Volley – Smoke, Confusion, and Casualties

At the instant the first musket cracked, the green erupted. It felt as if time itself split—a moment ago, tension held everything in place; now, the world dissolved into thunder, smoke, and shrieks. The initial report echoed across the grass, followed by a staccato flurry of shots from both sides. Columns of redcoats fired in disciplined volleys, muzzle flashes piercing the haze. Militia muskets answered, but not always in coordinated lines—some fired as they ran, others dropped their weapons in fright or confusion. Black powder smoke billowed outward, swallowing faces and forms in dirty gray clouds. The tang of burnt sulfur filled every breath. Within seconds, the air became thick, and vision was reduced to vague shapes moving among the noise.

Eyewitnesses described a nightmare. Ebenezer Munroe, a Lexington militiaman, remembered the sharp agony of being fired upon almost before he realized what was happening. "I returned fire," he later stated, "but the smoke and confusion made it impossible to see who was shooting." The sound was overwhelming—cracking muskets, shouted orders, screams from wounded men and terrified bystanders. You would have heard frantic shouts of warning, pained groans, and the thud of bodies falling to earth. Mothers in nearby homes grabbed children and ducked behind walls. Some ran to windows and saw neighbors staggering or crawling away from the volley. Even men trained for such chaos found themselves stunned by the sheer violence unleashed in those few seconds.

The casualties fell in grim patterns that local records would later trace in detail. Jonas Parker, a steadfast figure near the front, famously refused to leave his ground even as redcoats charged. He tried to reload but was struck by a British musket ball and fell where he stood—accounts say he was bayoneted as he reached for his musket again. Prince Estabrook, an enslaved man serving in the militia, took a bullet as well; he survived his wounds but carried the scars for life. Others dropped along the edge of the green or near Buckman Tavern, some struck while trying to flee toward safety. The dead and wounded formed a trail stretching from Parker's position past the meetinghouse and toward the homes at the green's edge. Each location tells its own story: a musket lying abandoned in wet grass, a bloodstain marking where resolve met steel and powder.

The breakdown of command was almost immediate. In those chaotic moments, orders became indistinguishable from panic. Militia lines, never rigid to begin with, scattered in all directions as men saw friends fall beside them or heard British bayonets clattering close behind. Some tried to rally near Buckman Tavern but found themselves blocked by frightened townsmen or stampeding livestock. Others bolted behind fences or into nearby woods, desperate for cover from relentless fire. The British pressed forward, some officers struggling to restrain their men as rage and adrenaline surged. For a handful of seconds, discipline collapsed—redcoats charged at retreating militia, some firing into backs, others slashing with bayonets.

The engagement lasted less than two minutes, but felt infinitely longer to those trapped within it. The panic spread not only among combatants but across the entire village green. Bystanders—men too old to fight or boys who had slipped out to watch—dove for cover or sprinted for safety as musket balls whistled past their heads. The shouts of British officers became lost in the uproar; the militiamen's voices grew hoarse from calling for help or warning others to run. Even seasoned soldiers found themselves unmoored by the turmoil—one British private later wrote that he could barely remember what happened once firing started; all recollection dissolved into noise and confusion.

When the smoke finally began to drift away and gunfire faded, bodies dotted the ground where minutes earlier neighbors had stood together in tense silence. Jonas Parker's body lay not far from where he had refused to retreat; Prince Estabrook groaned nearby, clutching his wound. Seven colonists died outright on Lexington Green that morning, with several more wounded, some severely enough never to recover fully. Local records and family memories would mark each spot where blood soaked into spring grass.

In those short moments, discipline gave way to disaster, fear replaced order, and the ordinary lives of a small village were forever changed by violence no one could control or truly comprehend. The volley on Lexington Green stands as a moment when confusion triumphed over command, and fate overran every intention set by leaders on both sides, leaving only casualties and questions behind.

Civilians on the Green – Wounded, Witnesses, and Family Loss

When the smoke finally thinned and the chaos of the volley faded, the green revealed a harrowing tableau that stretched far beyond the circle of armed men. You would have found women and children pressed to windows, faces painted with terror and disbelief, their morning routines shattered by violence. Some watched as their sons, fathers, or husbands fell in the grass, and others waited in dread for the gunfire to stop before daring to step outside. The elderly, unable to flee or fight, bore silent witness from doorways and porches, their memories of quieter days forever tainted. These non-combatants held a unique vantage—close enough to see every detail, powerless to intervene. Among these voices was Ruth Harrington, whose husband Jonathan fell that morning. Local accounts record how she watched as he staggered from the green, wounded but alive, crawling through blood and mud, striving for home. He collapsed just steps from his own door, reaching out for Ruth before he died. Her testimony later recounted that she wept over him in the doorway, sunlight glinting on his lifeless hand, the sound of musket fire still echoing in her ears.

Children experienced the tragedy from behind fragile glass. Some later recalled how their mothers pulled them back from windows as bullets splintered the frames. Others described hiding under beds or behind heavy furniture, listening to the shouts and gunshots with a mix of fear and curiosity. One young girl wrote years later about seeing her father fall and watching her mother run onto the green before all danger had passed. The trauma etched itself deeply—children who saw their neighbors shot would carry those images for decades. For many, this was their first taste of war: not tales of glory, but a grim spectacle played out on familiar ground.

The violence shattered more than bodies. It broke the sense of safety that had once defined Lexington. Families emerged as soon as the firing ceased—wives running to husbands, mothers searching for sons. The green became a field hospital and a place of mourning in the same instant. Women tended to the wounded where they lay, using whatever cloth or water they could find. Some risked musket balls still flying or bayonets flashing to reach loved ones. They pressed hands on wounds, whispered prayers, and called for neighbors to bring help. The deaths struck hardest where kinship ran thickest. Jonathan Harrington's final effort to crawl home became a symbol of loss for the town; his blood stained the threshold as his wife knelt beside him.

Bystanders became first responders with no warning or preparation. Townswomen dragged fallen men toward shelter as best they could. Some tried to staunch bleeding with torn aprons or offer water from buckets hauled up in haste. Elderly men gathered tools and planks, improvising stretchers to carry the most gravely hurt away from the open green. Others comforted the dying with psalms or held candles as dusk approached. The community's grief began even as smoke lingered over the grass.

Eyewitness testimony from these civilians shaped how Lexington remembered that morning. Local histories preserve quotes from women who described the terror of hearing shots so close to home and from children who never forgot the sight of bodies left on their family's lawn. These accounts often noted which homes became makeshift infirmaries or morgues, which neighbors braved a return to the green before it was truly safe, and how silence replaced chaos once the British moved on. The voices of these non-combatants offer stark evidence that war spares no one.

The psychological toll rippled outward. In the hours after the gunfire stopped, Lexington's church bells tolled in slow, somber cadence—a sound both familiar and newly dreadful. Each peal marked a life lost. Families gathered at meetinghouses not only for comfort but also to ask what they could do next; fear gave way to anger as news of deaths spread from house to house. Shock quickly transformed into resolve among many townsfolk—those who had watched in helplessness now swore never again to stand idle in the face of threat.

Communal rituals adapted with grim efficiency. Women washed blood from doorsteps and clothing; elders coordinated burials for those who died where they stood. Neighbors who had once argued over fences or taxes now shared food and silence as they processed loss together. Grief became a collective act—mourning interwoven with vows that Lexington would not forget nor forgive what had happened on its green.

The aftermath reached beyond Lexington itself. Messengers carried stories of civilian suffering to surrounding towns, spreading not just facts but emotion: shock, anger, a sense that something irreparable had been done to families and community alike. For many who survived that day— whether fighting or hiding—the violence brought an awakening that transformed private sorrow into public determination. The simple act of tolling bells echoed for miles, calling others to witness and respond to the tragedy that began with a single volley and ended with families forever changed.

The Immediate Aftermath – Medical Aid, Mourning, and British Decisions

As the smoke drifted away and the gunfire ceased, the green transformed from a place of battle into a landscape of stunned silence. British officers, shaken by the sudden violence, moved with urgency to restore discipline among their ranks. Some soldiers stood wide-eyed, clutching muskets, while others paced anxiously, awaiting orders. Major Pitcairn and Lieutenant Colonel Smith barked commands to reassemble the scattered companies, their voices sharp and unwavering. The regulars regrouped in columns, some glancing back at the bodies and wounded left behind. Their discipline reasserted itself not out of calm but necessity—they had a mission to finish and orders to follow. Officers checked their men for injuries, made quick counts, and pressed them to prepare for the march toward Concord. The moment for reflection was brief; duty demanded movement.

On the colonial side, chaos gave way to a different kind of action. Militiamen who had survived the volley rushed to help fallen friends. Several men dragged wounded comrades from open ground to the shelter of nearby homes or barns. Some moved with grim efficiency, others with shaking hands and tear-streaked faces. The townspeople streamed onto the green as soon as it was safe—women leading the way, children trailing behind, elders lending support wherever they could. There was no system, only instinct and community. Inside kitchens or parlors, they laid out the wounded on rough-hewn tables or beds, improvising care with what little they had.

Medical treatment in those first minutes was as basic as it was desperate. Local women became nurses by necessity, tending to bleeding wounds with strips of linen torn from aprons or bedsheets. They washed injuries with cool water drawn from wells and packed musket wounds with whatever clean rags were at hand. Some wounds were shallow—grazes or flesh wounds along arms and legs—while others were far more severe. Musket balls shattered bones, tore through muscle, or lodged deep in chests and abdomens. For those gravely injured, pain was constant and relief sparse. Whiskey or rum numbed agony for a time; herbal poultices offered scant comfort. Relatives hovered close by, whispering prayers or offering words of comfort. No one in Lexington had formal training as a surgeon; experience came from tending farm accidents or childhood fevers. Still, compassion and determination filled the gaps left by skill. Even British soldiers left wounded on the green received what help could be given—Lexington's people did not turn away from suffering, regardless of uniform.

Mourning began almost at once. As word spread through town, families gathered in clusters inside homes or on porches, searching for news of loved ones. The dead were carried gently from the grass—bodies wrapped in blankets or laid out on doors taken from hinges. Neighbors worked together to prepare each man for burial, washing blood from faces and straightening limbs with care. The rituals were simple but deeply felt: candles burned low in windows, psalms were murmured in hushed voices, and small groups assembled for prayers over each fallen man. Some families recited passages from well-worn Bibles; others simply wept and held each other. There was no time for an elaborate ceremony, but dignity mattered deeply. Every gesture honored the sacrifice made.

In this atmosphere of grief and confusion, British leadership faced hard decisions. Major Pitcairn and Lieutenant Colonel Smith understood that their mission—to reach Concord before Patriot resistance could organize—was not yet complete. Despite the shock of bloodshed on Lexington Green, orders remained unchanged: press forward without delay. Officers conferred quickly on the road's edge, weighing their situation. The dead and wounded were noted but not allowed to slow progress; any hesitation might allow more militia to gather ahead. Smith issued brisk instructions—close ranks, check powder (as ammunition had already been spent), and march west at once.

The mood among British ranks was tense but resolute. Soldiers' faces showed strain—some pale with fear, others set with anger or regret—but discipline took precedence over personal feeling. No one lingered on what had happened; training pushed them onward toward Concord. For many regulars, the encounter at Lexington was their first taste of combat outside Europe—a jolt that would linger long after the march resumed.

Lexington itself remained frozen in a strange twilight between war and mourning as the British column moved away. Families finished their vigils, neighbors carried out burials with heavy hearts, and those who survived promised never to forget what they had seen or lost.

This moment—raw with loss and decision—reshaped Lexington forever and sent ripples through every village between Boston and Concord. What began as a confrontation on a village green now spread outward, carrying new urgency and resolve across Massachusetts. As British troops marched toward their next objective, the day's true meaning had only just begun to reveal itself. The story now shifts westward—where news of bloodshed will meet new resistance at Concord's bridges and fields.

Congratulations! You've made it this far!

I hope you're enjoying *Lexington and Concord: The First Shots of Freedom*, and that you continue reading the rest of it…

Many potential readers consider the quality and quantity of reviews a book has earned, and the better the reviews, the more a seller prioritizes it.

All you have to do is locate this book online, scroll down to where it says "Write a customer review," and follow the directions to write a much-appreciated review. It doesn't have to be long. They recommend at least a few sentences.

Thanks much in advance.

Please keep reading,

Blake Whitworth

Chapter 5: The March to Concord Skirmishes, Bridges, and Turning Points

6:00–7:00 a.m. – British Advance Resumes

As the British column stands west of Lexington, the dawn brings tension that is almost palpable. Many soldiers already bear the marks of fatigue and the morning's violence—red coats stained, brows slick with sweat and powder, nerves on edge from the gunfire still echoing in memory. Lieutenant Colonel Smith, voice steady but urgent, relays General Gage's order: press on at all costs to Concord. Officers re-form the ranks, bayonets glint, and discipline reasserts itself through routine despite the shaken soldiers—some glancing back where friends fell, others clutching muskets as an act of courage.

Smith is clear: advance, regardless of losses. This is real combat for many—no longer the confident advance of an unstoppable force, but individuals confronting fear, adrenaline, and exhaustion. British privates later recall shaking hands and rattled nerves; one writes home of a morning that deeply unsettled him. Yet, months of drill and duty keep them moving, boots thudding in rhythm—a collective effort to overcome uncertainty.

But they are not alone. Along the twisting roads to Concord, colonial militia quietly gather just out of sight. The nighttime alarm has spread: men from Lincoln, Bedford, Acton, and other towns quickly position themselves along the route, having left fields, forges, and workshops behind. Militia companies are small—dozens at most—but their numbers grow with each mile. Muskets are varied, many powder horns carved with initials and dates, but determination binds these men more than any uniform.

Skirmishes erupt as soon as the British near Concord. At Meriam's Corner—where the road turns past homes and barns—local militia occupy high ground, watching for redcoats. The British advance cautiously, recalling disasters like Munroe Tavern, conscious now of ambush at every turn. Firing comes from behind fences or hedges—nothing like a pitched battle, but brief, tense exchanges that fray nerves on both sides. These are flashes of violence: a shot, a disciplined reply, quick movement, then silence punctuated by hurried footsteps and low voices.

Every landmark takes on new meaning—Meriam's Corner becomes a rallying point; Brooks Hill, ahead, is both obstacle and hope for those trying to delay the British. Simple map names become fraught with the weight of decisions being made—fight or retreat, risk or flee.

The psychological strain mounts mile after mile. British troops scan every window and shadow; exhaustion weighs heavy—many have not slept, and some are wounded. Seasoned officers mutter anxiously about being surrounded or cut off. Letters home describe the "dreadful uncertainty" and "faces at every door." Colonials, meanwhile, are driven by a different urgency—a sense that everything dear to them lies just ahead, at risk.

Colonial accounts reflect this. One Acton volunteer feels both fear and duty burning inside; another sees his company moving through Concord meadows "like a river swelling with every tributary"—each man's presence only hardening their resolve. Along the road between Lexington and Concord, both sides press on: British soldiers driven by command, colonists answering a deeper call.

Entering Concord – Search for Hidden Weapons and Supplies

The British column entered Concord urgently yet cautiously, their discipline partially restored after the confusion at Lexington. Officers, armed with Loyalist-supplied lists and maps showing suspected arms caches, divided detachments to target the town center, South Bridge, and most critically, Colonel James Barrett's outlying farm. Each group advanced deliberately, muskets ready, wary of attack and the silent stares from townspeople.

The soldiers began sweeping public buildings—meetinghouses, storehouses—using maps, crowbars, and a cautious eye on civilians. They uncovered barrels and gun carriages, but much proved ordinary: flour mistaken for powder, farm tools for cannon parts. Residents, meanwhile, watched from fences and windows—mothers gathered children, neighbors whispered updates, all alert and guarded.

British squads combed Concord's homes and outlying farms, sometimes politely, often forcefully. Most families had acted earlier: valuables and arms hidden under floorboards, in cellars, or spirited to neighbors in the night. At Barrett's farm, soldiers dug up freshly turned earth, finding only dirt and discarded tools—clear evidence of hasty removal, but not the sought-after supplies.

Frustration grew as promising leads repeatedly ended in empty hiding places or clever ruses. One officer described his "vexation of false leads" when every barn and shed yielded only farm supplies. Trust between soldiers and townspeople eroded further with every fruitless search—sometimes a musket surfaced behind a chimney, more often just linens or Bibles. The pattern was clear: Concord's residents had worked fast and well to safeguard their stores.

Their success relied on relentless effort and unity. Farmers hauled powder deep into woodland before dawn; boys ferried musket parts to distant farms under cloaks; women hid supplies in baskets appearing to hold nothing but food. Entire families sometimes vanished into the countryside, returning only after the search. These maneuvers reflected coordination by local leaders who knew both the land and the stakes.

Women played a pivotal role. With many men away, mothers and daughters moved supplies and acted as lookouts. Children signaled the British approach with handkerchiefs or songs, and bore warning messages along secret orchard paths. Few soldiers questioned the innocence of a mother's bread basket, not knowing cartridges or flints lay within.

Despite these efforts, the British did uncover and destroy some military stores—gun carriages, a few barrels labeled as gunpowder, and the odd arms cache too heavy to move. Still, the amount captured was far less than expected, frustrating officers who had anticipated an easy rebel defeat. Instead, they faced clear signs of resourcefulness and resolve—freshly dug fields, emptied barns—a testament to Concord's strategic preparation.

The tension was mutual. Families hid from windows or hillsides, some weeping at destruction, some relieved at what remained safely hidden. Suspicion and anxiety were everywhere; a British sergeant called Concord "this sullen town," while a local farmer feared that each step might reveal a secret store.

Every moment reflected this standoff—soldiers seeking proof of rebel defiance, townsfolk determined to conceal it. Across New England, this pattern repeated as the alarm spread.

The North Bridge Standoff – Colonial Militias Converge

By mid-morning, new sounds signaled a changing battle. Militia from Acton, Lincoln, Bedford, and other towns assembled at a rise by the North Bridge over the slow Concord River, shifting the balance of power with their growing numbers. Major John Buttrick and Colonel James Barrett rallied these units into a coordinated force. Acton's resolute men, Lincoln and Bedford's contingents, all formed ranks along the river.

British officers moved quickly to fortify both bridge ends, ordering light infantry to hold the crossing until the supply search was complete. Redcoats formed shallow ranks, muskets loaded, warily facing the swelling colonial crowd.

A tense stand-off followed. Colonial leaders debated: wait for reinforcements or press the British before more destruction? Buttrick, insisting on unity and restraint—fire only if fired upon—pushed his men to be ready.

Signaling and intent became dangerously unclear. A British officer misconstrued colonial movements as surrender, while colonials feared any advance would prompt British attack. The stalemate broke when Buttrick shouted, "Fire, fellow soldiers—for God's sake, fire!" Both sides exchanged volleys almost simultaneously in the tight confines—a narrow bridge with opposing ranks barely seventy yards apart.

The confrontation was short but momentous: the first return fire by colonial forces against British regulars in formation, marking an escalation no one could undo.

"The Shot Heard 'Round the World" – Fact, Legend, and the Moment

As the smoke settled, the events at North Bridge quickly passed into legend. Eyewitnesses saw Acton's Isaac Davis, shot through the heart, fall at the front of his company; Abner Hosmer was another early casualty. British accounts mention "great confusion" as men scrambled for cover under fire.

Official reports differ—some colonials claimed they only fired after being attacked, while a few British officers insisted the first shot came from behind the willows. Historians remain divided on the precise sequence.

Yet the wider impact was clear: this clash was soon immortalized as "the shot heard 'round the world," thanks to Emerson's "Concord Hymn." At later centennials and commemorations, the story was retold and mythologized.

Agreed facts: Davis and Hosmer were killed instantly, redcoats retreated in haste, colonials pressed forward—transforming a tense faceoff into open war.

British and Colonial Perspectives – Orders, Misunderstandings, and Fear

After North Bridge, chaos swept both forces. Lieutenant Colonel Smith struggled to rally scattered British units, shifting from the search for supplies to urgent defense and retreat amid rumors of mass colonial reinforcements.

Within colonial ranks, there was debate over pursuing British forces or consolidating their gains. Communication was confused—runners relayed conflicting news about casualties and orders.

Fear caused rash actions—a jumpy British private shot a farmer near a stone wall, mistaking him for a scout. Some soldiers, hungry and weary, broke discipline to loot for food, further angering townspeople.

Personal letters record the tension—a sergeant writing home described "dreadful confusion," while a Concord militiaman felt both "strange joy and terror."

Civilians in Concord – Safeguarding Homes and Livelihoods

For Concord's civilians, survival took courage and ingenuity. Women hid valuables and important papers in wells, beneath stones, or under haystacks, sometimes risking discovery. Children were sent to distant farms for safety.

Some residents watched from attics, like Mary Hartwell, glimpsing musket flashes from her window, while others rescued wounded militia from the fields. Quiet resistance included misdirecting British patrols, hiding supplies, or using children as messengers.

The day left immediate scars: homes damaged, gardens trampled, livestock scattered. Material losses were logged in later compensation petitions, but town records also capture stories of trauma, resilience, and rebuilding—a testament to Concord's endurance as smoke cleared from the battlefields of April 19th.

The North Bridge Standoff – Colonial Militias Converge

Word of the alarm spread fast across the countryside. By mid-morning, the roads and fields around Concord swelled with men from Acton, Lincoln, Bedford, and other nearby towns. Most were not soldiers, but farmers, millers, apprentices, and tradesmen, many still wearing work clothes under their homespun coats. As these small groups assembled into a mass outside Concord, their collective presence radically shifted the balance. Neighbors and strangers alike united under the threat, forming a force larger than any one town could have managed.

Major John Buttrick and Colonel James Barrett quickly filled leadership roles. Buttrick gave clear orders and brought cohesion to volunteers who had never drilled together. Barrett, motivated in part by the threat to his own farm, offered authority and local expertise. The officers organized the arriving companies onto the hillside above the river—Acton men with Isaac Davis out front, quiet but eager; Lincoln's men known for their discipline; Bedford's group bolstering numbers and order. Officers checked powder, offered last advice, and whispered encouragement.

Across the Concord River, British light infantry guarded both ends of the North Bridge, tasked with holding the crossing until their search parties returned from Barrett's farm. The redcoats formed tight ranks—two companies defending each approach, muskets loaded and bayonets fixed. They were outnumbered and aware of their exposed position; discipline and firepower were their only advantages. British officers kept a sharp watch for any sign of colonial movement.

As militia numbers grew, tension mounted. Men eyed one another, silently wondering if they were truly ready to fight regular troops in open ground. Colonial officers debated whether to advance on the bridge or hold back. Some warned an attack might trigger disaster, while others feared delay would let the British destroy vital supplies or push further into Concord. Each new arrival added strength but also confusion, with questions of command and purpose swirling.

Amid the din, signals and shouted orders were often misread. At one point, a British officer reportedly mistook colonial movements for a surrender and lowered his pistol, only to realize his error as Buttrick's men pressed forward. On the colonial side, British maneuvers looked like preparations for burning more buildings or seizing civilians. Each misinterpretation ratcheted up the risk, making restraint harder each minute.

The landscape amplified the tension. The North Bridge spanned a slow river between muddy, willow-lined banks. On one side stood Buttrick and Davis with their militia; on the other, British light infantry braced for attack. The distance between opponents was painfully short—barely seventy yards—leaving little room for error. Accounts from both sides note how clearly men could see faces across the water. The bridge itself offered no cover; anyone crossing would be fully exposed.

Suddenly, Buttrick's order rang out: "Fire, fellow soldiers, for God's sake, fire!" This command followed a British volley that killed Davis at the front of Acton's line. The order broke the final tension; colonial muskets answered almost as one, their shots echoing off the stone and water.

Smoke quickly obscured the field, turning the chaotic scene into a confusion of shouts, pain, and desperate movements for cover.

Later maps would precisely mark where each company stood: Acton men closest to the bridge, Lincoln and Bedford companies behind on higher ground, British infantry in tight ranks guarding both approaches. The sightlines were clear—anyone lifting a musket could scarcely miss those across the span. Bullet impacts splintered bridge rails and kicked up dirt at soldiers' feet.

In those few crucial minutes at North Bridge, dynamics changed for everyone present and for observers far beyond. The coordinated militias under steady leaders faced disciplined but isolated British troops, with a series of fatal miscommunications pushing both sides to the brink. The standoff was not just a firefight; it marked the moment when ordinary people demonstrated they could organize and challenge imperial power on their own terms—a moment that turned the course of history, witnessed by hundreds who held their breath beside the muddy riverbank.

The Shot Heard 'Round the World" – Fact, Legend, and the Moment

Standing by the Concord River, picturing the North Bridge that April morning, you sense the tense confrontation. On one side, British light infantry; on the other, colonial militiamen facing regular troops in combat for the first time. The air carried the chill, the scent of gunpowder and river mud, urgent voices, and shouted commands. Suddenly, gunfire shattered the morning calm. In a brief, confused volley, Isaac Davis of Acton was shot in the heart, and Abner Hosmer fell beside him—ordinary men whose deaths would gain lasting significance. Witnesses described chaos: blue smoke swirling, cries and commands, as colonials pressed across the bridge. British troops recounted seeing flashes from the American side; others said it was impossible to know who truly fired first.

Accounts conflicted. Some colonials swore the British fired first, pointing to the casualties; British officers claimed the opposite, accusing the militia of shooting from behind cover. Actually, panic ruled—noise, smoke, and confusion blurred everything. Modern historians have sifted through these reports, comparing positions and timings. Their reconstructions suggest the firing was nearly simultaneous, with nerves and confusion turning tension into violence. Once a shot rang out on that narrow bridge, instinct took over, and both sides joined battle.

After those first shots, the British reeled, retreating frantically toward Concord, some leaving supplies and wounded behind. For many redcoats, the moment was a shock—unexpected resistance, casualties, and confusion. Retreat was chaotic, not organized, with fearful letters home reflecting that terror. On the colonial side, the shock was equally deep. The militiamen who fired stopped, stunned by the enormity—they had crossed from protest to war. Many recalled a stunned quiet after the volley, as the significance of their actions settled over them.

Word spread rapidly that blood had been shed at the North Bridge. As time passed, the incident shifted from a confused skirmish to a legendary moment. Emerson's "Concord Hymn," penned for the 1837 monument dedication, immortalized it as "the shot heard 'round the world." His poetic phrase elevated real confusion into myth, transforming a local tragedy into a symbol of global revolutions. Emerson's words are now inscribed on monuments and recited at commemorations.

Over the decades, North Bridge's story evolved with retelling. By the 1875 centennial, Americans flocked to Concord to honor fallen militiamen with speeches and ceremonies. Children repeated tales of farmers defying tyranny; textbooks celebrated liberty's victory over empire. The 1975 bicentennial blended reenactment and pride: thousands gathered, some in period dress, focusing on the legend more than lingering questions. Ceremony blurred fact and myth as anniversary after anniversary honored the event, often glossing over the uncertainties of that initial encounter.

Yet, questions persist. Original accounts contradict one another: colonial depositions insist militia held their fire until struck, while British officers accused colonists of firing first. Some recall an accidental trigger or a nervous shot; others suggest intentional aggression. Modern historians generally agree that the sequence can never be perfectly known, lost to noise, confusion, and adrenaline in those seconds.

What is certain is that at North Bridge, ordinary men had to make split-second, fateful decisions. The aftermath was not joyful but sobering—British in retreat, colonists stunned by their own actions. Both sides knew, in that instant, life would never return to what it had been.

Fact vs. Legend Sidebar

- Fact: Isaac Davis and Abner Hosmer died leading their company across North Bridge; British soldiers fell or retreated under fire.
- Fact: Eyewitnesses from both sides disagreed on who shot first.
- Legend: Emerson's "shot heard 'round the world" created a poetic epic from what was likely a moment of chaos.
- Fact: Historians remain divided—modern reconstructions cannot identify whose musket cracked first.

Emerson's enduring phrase remains not for its accuracy, but because it voices a shared need: to see the revolution's origins in a single moment of bravery and consequence on a muddy bridge, an echo from Massachusetts rippling across the world.

British and Colonial Perspectives – Orders, Misunderstandings, and Fear

North of Concord, the atmosphere was tense and chaotic after the fighting at North Bridge. British officers, shaken and wounded, struggled to regroup their scattered troops.

Lieutenant Colonel Smith, despite his injuries, tried to impose order, calling for a headcount and searching for missing officers amid confusion. His aides relayed instructions, but many soldiers barely understood or even heard them. Men whispered anxiously, checked wounds, and counted their dwindling ammunition while casting worried glances at the growing colonial presence across the river. Redcoats took cover behind stone walls and wagons, nervously keeping watch for fresh attacks.

British diaries and letters captured the chaos. A sergeant described "dreadful confusion," where orders, rumors, and pleas from the wounded mixed together. Officers' faces betrayed deep uncertainty, as no one could accurately predict what might happen next. Wild rumors circulated that thousands of rebels were approaching, and this fear intensified as couriers reported seeing columns of militia on distant roads. Officers debated whether to stay and fight or retreat, unsure if their mission even mattered anymore.

The colonial side was also marked by confusion and difficult choices. Militia leaders met under maples near the river, arguing quietly over whether to press the British or adopt a defensive stance. Some wanted to seize the moment and pursue the retreating redcoats, while others suspected a trap and urged caution. Fresh reinforcements—muddy and exhausted—arrived with wild stories, some claiming more British were on the way, others even suggesting Boston was burning. These unconfirmed tales fueled both hope and anxiety. Some men took positions along stone walls, not knowing if more fighting was imminent, while others reloaded behind brush, nervous and trembling.

Communication faltered on both sides. Orders became garbled as they passed from man to man, numbers of enemy troops were exaggerated or minimized, and rumors flourished. A single musket shot might trigger panic, its meaning unclear. British scouts sent down side roads often didn't return or brought no news, which heightened unease. Even Smith's second-in-command hesitated to dispatch more patrols, fearing more men would be lost to unseen opponents in the countryside.

Misunderstandings led to dangerous incidents. A jumpy British private, mistaking a local farmer for a rebel, fired upon him—fortunately missing, but terrifying the man. In other cases, hungry or panicked soldiers raided empty homes for supplies, taking whatever they could find; one group seized a basket from a fleeing child, only to find it contained apples and homemade cartridges. Such actions were usually not ordered, but discipline often broke down amid fear and hunger.

Colonial anxieties echoed these British fears, though mixed with exhilaration. A Concord militiaman described a "strange joy and terror" watching the redcoats retreat; it seemed incredible that local men had stood up to regular British troops. Another militiaman remembered his heart pounding as he waited for orders, not knowing if he'd survive or lose his home to retreating soldiers. Men along the road clung to rumors—some cheered at reports of

British losses, others worried about stories of farms burning or neighbors shot by mistake.

British morale sank further into dread. Letters from junior officers' homes were filled with fear. One lieutenant admitted he shook so badly after hearing about rebel forces at Meriam's Corner that he could hardly hold his sword. Every face was potentially an enemy, every shadow a threat. The possibility of disaster loomed with every move.

Both sides operated in a fog of uncertainty and rumor. Neither Smith nor the colonial commanders truly knew the scale of forces against them, nor what would come next. Panic and fear shaped every choice—hesitation when boldness was required, impulsive action when patience was needed. Orders went unheeded or misunderstood; messages were lost or twisted.

In the wake of North Bridge, both armies were left unsettled. British soldiers were gripped by fear and doubt; colonials buzzed with anxious excitement, neither side sure whether they had achieved victory or were simply caught up in the beginnings of a war that would forever change their world.

Civilians in Concord – Safeguarding Homes and Livelihoods

When news reached Concord that British regulars were approaching, townspeople responded with a mix of fear and determination. Women led efforts to defend homes: valuables like silver, candlesticks, and rings quickly vanished from sight, being hidden under floorboards, beneath hearthstones, or in barns. Family bibles, deeds, wills, and precious letters were tucked into flour barrels or buried in gardens, their hiding spots known only to a trusted few. Some women sent valuables to neighbors on back roads, exchanging both items and whispered reassurances. Mothers pressed coins into children's hands, sending them to distant relatives with strict instructions to avoid main roads and windows. For the children, these hurried journeys brought confusion, fear, and occasional excitement as they joined cousins in secluded farmhouses, listening anxiously for any signs of battle from town.

Older children sometimes carried more than just their own belongings—coats stuffed with silver buttons and pockets heavy with family heirlooms grew common as families split up for safety. One parent might remain behind to tend animals or defend the property while the other led the young to safety, hearts heavy but hopeful that separation would offer protection.

Some civilians could not bring themselves to hide or flee. Mary Hartwell, for instance, watched the unfolding events from her attic, determined to witness and remember as redcoats crossed the bridge, smoke rose, and neighbors dashed for cover. Though shaken, she later shared her account, preserving the memory of the day's violence and courage.

Others stayed close to the action, risking their lives to help the wounded. Farmers who lingered behind fences rushed injured militia to kitchens and barns for improvised care, offering soaked linen for wounds and food to the weakened. Some even braved gunfire to drag the fallen to safety, risking their own lives without hesitation.

Resistance often took quieter forms. Concord women devised clever ways to mislead the British during their searches. Messages for militia leaders might be hidden inside a loaf of bread or a basket carried by a child. When questioned by soldiers, housewives might feign ignorance or direct them to places where nothing would be found. Even a child's song or a colored scarf could be used as a signal. These small acts of deception and sabotage— loosening barn planks, scattering tools, relaying information—were rooted in quick thinking and solidarity.

Such resistance did not come without cost. Homes bore visible scars: broken windows from musket balls, doors forced open, furniture smashed by searching soldiers. Flower beds were trampled, orchards stripped, food seized, livestock scattered or killed, fences torn down for barricades, and barns left damaged or burned.

The aftermath was harsh. Families inventoried their losses: missing silver, ruined books, scorched outbuildings, and supplies seized. Official claims listed everything from flour to horses lost during the chaos, reflecting not only the material but also the emotional cost—trauma that persisted for months. Children who saw violence would remember it for life; parents mourned their lost sense of safety.

Despite this, the rebuilding began quickly. Neighbors shared tools and seed, women patched fences and baked bread for those in need, and men worked cooperatively to restore barns and mills. Community meetings took on a somber tone as residents planned recovery efforts and urged unity in the face of adversity.

Out of the grief, resilience grew. The events of April 19 forged a new sense of unity and determination. Concord's civilians, strengthened by shared sacrifices, became an inspiring example for others across Massachusetts to defend their own rights and families.

With homes damaged and hearts shaken, Concord's people moved forward together—undaunted by their losses, newly resolved to face whatever lay ahead. Their story marked not just personal tragedy but the beginning of a shared struggle, as news spread, public opinion shifted, and the road toward open revolution became inevitable.

Chapter 6: The Long Retreat Ambush, Retribution, and Desperation

Noon – Panic Sets In: The British Begin Their Retreat

The midday sun burns down on the dusty roads west of Boston as the battered British column stands silent in Concord's shadow. Rt. Col. Smith, wounded and pale, gives a crisp command: retreat. Officers, already fraying at the edges, hurry to relay the order, but discipline—shaken by the morning's volleys at Lexington and Concord Bridge—begins to disintegrate. Conflicting orders echo, young privates look anxiously to their sergeants, and the first shots from pursuing militia crack out behind them. The threat is no longer abstract; danger presses in from all sides.

Fatigue weighs heavily. Most soldiers haven't eaten since before dawn, canteens are empty, and lips cracked with thirst. Powder blackens their faces, torn uniforms bear stains of mud. Many clutch near-empty cartridge boxes—some have only a single charge left. Hunger erodes discipline; exhaustion causes more than one man to stumble behind his company. Officers, nerves shredded by chaos and loss, strain their hoarse voices trying to maintain order.

Discipline is on the brink of collapse. The once-precise lines move in anxious clusters, muskets heavy and burdensome. Panic simmers—every sound sets nerves jangling. The landscape itself feels hostile; any stone wall, tree stand, or barn might conceal enemies. Some mutter prayers, others grasp for English training that now feels meaningless in this strange countryside.

The challenges for British command are daunting. Smith's wound hampers his leadership, so Major Pitcairn takes on extra duties but can barely make himself heard over the growing musket fire. Restoring order is nearly impossible: the rutted, narrow colonial road stretches almost a mile, winding through thickets and dips that break the line of sight and frustrate communication. Horses slip or refuse to advance under fire; wagons become obstacles when damaged. Every leadership failure risks triggering disaster.

The route from Concord village to Meriam's Corner is treacherous. The road curves between open fields and tangled woods, often too narrow for more than two soldiers abreast. New militia companies—some fresh, some grim— arrive constantly, stationing themselves at bends and rises. When the British pass, the militia fire from cover and move, creating a sense of being surrounded and hounded. Each step forward means fresh threats from unseen enemies growing in number by the minute.

The sensation of entrapment intensifies. Redcoats spot glimpses of armed farmers in the fields or behind rocks. Shots ring out, smoke drifting from yet another ambush. At Meriam's Corner, where the road squeezes between swamps and farmhouses, the danger peaks as more colonial troops close escape routes and further disrupt the retreating column.

Meanwhile, officers make split-second choices: rally here, abandon wounded there, force through bottlenecks without waiting for the slowest. Even experienced leaders falter as fatigue and chaos mount. For many redcoats, the retreat is no organized withdrawal but a wild dash for survival— through unfamiliar territory, every stride dogged by relentless pursuit.

If you stood among them, you'd feel history not as a distant story, but as sweat burning your eyes, powder sting in your nose, and the sharp ache of fear at each barked command. The long retreat has begun, and none can know who will see Boston again, or how many names will soon be remembered only in mourning.

Colonial Pursuit – "The Road Was Lined with Fury"

As the British withdrew, the countryside came alive. Men from Reading, Billerica, Woburn, and beyond streamed in, armed and determined. Moving in loose groups or pairs, they didn't form lines but instead spread out along the road, vanishing into orchards, pastures, and barns for cover. The advantage tipped as redcoats moved exposed while militia slipped unseen through trees and thickets. Every bend or barn concealed another marksman. Colonial shooters fired from behind fences and barn doors, fleeing before British muskets could target them.

Militia communicated with speed and ingenuity—smoke signals, blasts on cow horns, even birdcalls coordinated their attacks. For the British, the retreat became a running gauntlet, offering no moments of rest. Once ordinary farmers became relentless hunters, cooperating with impressive agility. Small groups fired from cover and quickly melted away. These guerrilla tactics, once called "Indian-style," left redcoats bewildered and infuriated. British volleys were met by multiple shots from hidden colonial hands.

The fight intensified, especially past Brooks Hill and into the Bloody Angle, a sharp road turn lined with woods and fences. Here, fresh militia from new towns pressed the attack. Survivors reported musket balls from all directions, feeling trapped at each step forward. At Bloody Angle, some redcoats fell not just to muskets but to the rage of colonials avenging wounded friends. The pursuit left experienced British soldiers shaken—one wrote the road "was lined with fury," as constant attack broke their nerve.

Colonial anger drove this pursuit. Letters and accounts describe blood boiling at the sight of wounded neighbors— every shot fired for their people. The pursuit became more than defense; it was vengeance, a chance for colonists to wield power over the king's men for the first time, thrilling even the most cautious militia.

Flanking Maneuvers and Roadside Ambushes – Tactics Explained

Militia leaders knew head-on fighting was futile, so they sent flanking parties ahead through fields and lanes, attacking at every curve and choke point like Bloody Angle. These spots became deadly crossfire zones shielded by stone fences and woods. The British responded with bayonet charges and musket volleys to flush out attackers, but these desperate efforts succeeded only with heavy losses.

Confusion was widespread. Colonials sometimes fired at each other in the chaos. British officers struggled to gauge numbers, at times convinced thousands attacked when sometimes just dozens pressed forward. At Parker's Revenge, Lexington men ambushed the column from a rise and then quickly vanished, avoiding counterattack. Near present-day Arlington at the Foot of the Rocks, acts of local bravery stood out—a farmer risked his life to drag a wounded friend to safety while bullets tore the earth nearby.

Arrival at Charlestown – Exhaustion, Losses, and British Survival

By late afternoon, the battered British finally approached Charlestown. Bloodied, out of supplies, and exhausted, many soldiers limped or leaned on comrades. Some collapsed, others moved from sheer fear or willpower. Officers' faces betrayed defeat; ranks broke, and some soldiers wept openly from shock and exhaustion.

Rescue finally arrived with General Percy's fresh troops and artillery. Their disciplined lines shielded the survivors, and cannon fire forced the colonial pursuers to finally fall back as evening came over Prospect Hill and Bunker Hill. Seeing their muskets were no match for artillery, the colonists slipped away into the gathering dark—frustrated but alive. In Charlestown, British surgeons treated the wounded through the night among groans and whispered pleas.

The night was pierced by distant cries for aid. Casualty lists lengthened, and local burial grounds filled with the dead of both sides. Survivors wrote home in disbelief—missing neighbors, lost friends, and the shocking transformation of what had begun as an ordinary day.

House-to-House Conflict – Civilians Caught in the Crossfire

Along the retreat route from Concord through Menotomy, the violence of April 19 spilled directly into the lives and homes of ordinary families. Houses and farms, once symbols of safety, were transformed into battlegrounds. In Menotomy—what you now know as Arlington—windows shattered as musket balls tore through sashes and walls. The Jason Russell House stands out as a vivid example. Jason Russell, a local farmer with a bad leg, had decided to defend his home rather than flee. He believed the thick walls would shield his family and neighbors from stray shots. As the British column neared, he urged several militiamen to join him inside. The fighting outside quickly turned desperate. Bullets thudded into the siding and splintered doors; smoke from gunfire crept under thresholds.

Suddenly, British soldiers stormed the house. In the confusion, Russell was shot and bayoneted at his own doorstep, a fate shared by several militia who had sought shelter with him. Blood pooled on the floorboards—marks that, decades later, visitors would still see as grim reminders of the day's violence. Families in nearby homes heard every musket shot, each bang of a door or window carrying both fear and warning. Mothers rushed children into cellars or up narrow staircases, pressing hands over mouths to muffle sobs. Elders crouched in dark closets, praying for the shooting to end while glass tinkled down from above.

Eyewitnesses described the terror in plain terms. Bullets whistled through kitchens and bedrooms; heavy footsteps thundered upon stairs as soldiers searched for snipers or loot. A child watched through a crack in the shutters as redcoats fired blindly into barns, searching for hidden militiamen. In more than one home, food left half-eaten on the table was soon scattered across the floor by fleeing families or searching troops. The sense of invasion was total. For many, the day's events would become a permanent scar—recalled in nightmares and retold for generations.

Civilians faced impossible choices. Some fled across fields, dodging stray fire as they ran for distant neighbors' houses or into the woods. Others hid in cramped cellars for hours, listening to shouts and groans overhead. In homes where men had stayed behind to defend their property, tragedy often struck. Jason Russell's story was not unique—other men fell defending their thresholds or were wounded as they tried to shield loved ones. Women and older children found themselves suddenly cast as caretakers, tending broken bodies on makeshift beds of blankets and straw. Bandages were torn from petticoats; water fetched under fire.

Acts of bravery shone through the chaos. In one Menotomy home, a mother risked her life to drag a wounded militiaman from the yard into her kitchen, stanching his bleeding with strips of apron while her children hid beneath the table. Another woman, widowed only months before, guided her frail father into the root cellar, then crept upstairs with a lantern to warn others when it was momentarily safe to move. Some families shared their meager food and water with battered stragglers who stumbled to their doors seeking refuge.

The aftermath left an almost unrecognizable landscape inside many homes. Blood stains darkened wooden floors; broken glass crunched underfoot. Furniture was upended or smashed; family Bibles and precious heirlooms lay scattered among powder-blackened dishes. Pantries stood emptied—not only by desperate soldiers but also by families forced to flee in haste, abandoning bread and cheese to rot or be trampled. Clothing, bedding, and even livestock sometimes disappeared during the tumult, lost to looters or simply chaos.

Returning home after the fighting brought its own hardship. Families found not only physical wreckage but emotional wounds that ran deep. Children asked questions no parent could easily answer: why had soldiers come? Would they return? Mothers swept up glass and patched holes in plaster while fathers—if they made it back—inspected bullet-riddled barns and counted livestock. In the weeks that followed, townspeople filed official petitions for compensation with local authorities. These records—listing shattered windows, destroyed fences, missing food stores—became some of our most vivid evidence of what ordinary people endured.

The Jason Russell House itself became a somber symbol of civilian sacrifice and resilience. Eleven militia died there or nearby—the highest single-home toll that day—while two British soldiers also fell within its walls. Bullet holes in clapboards remained long after, a mute testimony to what had happened inside. Neighbors buried Russell and the others in the old burying ground, marking their graves with stones carved by trembling hands.

All along the retreat route, similar stories unfolded—some now lost to history except for a line in church records or a faded diary entry about "the day death came to our door." The violence did not discriminate; it struck wealthy merchants and poor farmers alike, old women and infants huddled under blankets together as war swept through their lives without warning or mercy. This day changed more than political boundaries; it altered families forever and left scars that no amount of time could fully erase.

Plundering and Retribution – The Controversy over British Conduct

As the British soldiers retreated through the villages and farmlands outside Boston, the fighting blurred the line between battlefield and home. The chaos of April 19th provided a grim opportunity for discipline to break down within the ranks. In Menotomy and Cambridge, property owners later described scenes of disorder and loss—looted pantries, barns stripped of livestock, and valuables snatched from mantelpieces or chests. Selectmen in these towns cataloged stolen or destroyed goods: barrels of flour vanished, silverware disappeared, and livestock were driven off or slaughtered in the yard. Even simple tools, family Bibles, and clothing were not spared. Some households found their bread ovens still smoldering from hasty meals cooked by passing soldiers; others discovered empty cider casks tipped over in the rush. The British, hungry and exhausted, often searched desperately for food, water, or shelter. Letters from redcoats themselves admit to snatching bread and cheese from kitchens, milking cows on the spot, or ransacking pantries. A private wrote of "scarcely a drop to drink," describing how he and his mates stormed through a farmhouse just to find a bucket of water. These moments reveal both the physical needs of men on the edge and the collapse of the strict order that had defined the morning's marches.

Officers attempted to restrain such behavior, shouting commands and even striking at their own men with flat blades or musket butts in vain efforts to restore order. Yet control slipped away amid the gunfire and confusion. The relentless pursuit by colonial militia put every officer on edge, often separating them from their companies and leaving small groups of redcoats isolated. When under fire, soldiers ignored orders and dashed into barns or houses for cover, sometimes tearing apart interiors in search of food, ammunition, or valuables. In some instances, entire rooms were left upended: plates shattered, beds overturned, and drawers emptied on the floor as redcoats searched frantically for anything useful or edible.

The reaction from the colonists was swift and unforgiving. Militia caught redcoats looting barns or hiding behind haystacks faced no mercy. Isolated soldiers were shot down in fields or dragged from hiding places without hope of quarter. In one Menotomy orchard, a group of British soldiers attempting to plunder livestock found themselves surrounded by armed farmers; none escaped alive. These retributive acts quickly escalated the violence well beyond the discipline of ordinary warfare. At times, wounded redcoats pleading for help were refused aid or even finished off by enraged militiamen who saw their own homes burning or ransacked nearby. The cycle was brutal and fast—each act of plundering fueled another act of vengeance.

News of these events traveled at astonishing speed across Massachusetts. Broadsides—single sheets posted on doors and tavern walls—recounted stories of "barbarities" committed by British troops: homes pillaged, women threatened, elders beaten in their own kitchens. Local newspapers ran testimonies from property owners and selectmen, listing what was lost or destroyed and sometimes tallying the dead livestock or broken furniture as evidence of British cruelty. These accounts did not remain local gossip; they soon reached Boston and beyond, inflaming public opinion throughout the colonies.

The power of atrocity stories lay not only in what they described but in how they rallied resistance. In every town that received these reports, ordinary people saw their own families reflected in the victims. Letters home spoke of outrage and sorrow; sermons thundered against "the ravages of tyranny." Even as far as Philadelphia or New York, readers encountered tales of burning homes and looted churches—events that transformed distant skirmishes into shared cause. Political leaders seized upon these reports to bolster recruitment and harden resolve. In town meetings and at muster grounds, speakers invoked the images of plundered homes as a call to arms.

British officers protested that such conduct did not reflect official policy. Some even issued statements denying any orders to loot or destroy private property, blaming instead the stress of combat and isolation from supplies. Yet few colonists believed these words; for them, the evidence was too immediate—scorched fields, empty larders, and blood on the threshold. In this climate of suspicion and outrage, every new rumor gained weight: a story of a silver spoon stolen in Cambridge might become a tale of mass destruction by the time it reached Worcester or Salem.

This legacy of plundering and retribution shaped how both sides remembered April 19th. For many British soldiers, the day stood as a shameful example of lost control and desperate acts committed under fire. For colonial families, it marked a turning point—a day when home became battleground, when neighbors defended each other not only with muskets but with memory and word. The battle for public opinion raged long after the smoke cleared from the fields around Boston. Accounts—real or exaggerated—spread through every colony, stoking anger and binding communities together against a common enemy. The scars left behind were not only physical but emotional, etched into family lore and local history for generations to come.

Flanking Maneuvers and Roadside Ambushes – Tactics Explained

The winding Massachusetts roads edged with stone fences and woods formed a battlefield that favored the colonial militia on April 19, 1775. Familiar with every pasture and hidden lane, these men used the landscape to their advantage. Their tactics, developed from hunting and farming experience, focused on ambush rather than open confrontation. Instead of lining up in fields, they spread into small bands, slipping ahead through cow paths and behind stone walls to set ambushes at bends like the "Bloody Angle." Each sharp turn became an opportunity for sudden musket fire before they melted away to set another trap further down the road.

These irregular tactics gave the militia a surprise advantage over British forces trained for traditional, linear warfare. Colonial flanking parties tried to isolate or encircle pieces of the British column, keeping redcoats constantly off balance. At road narrows or through wooded stretches, attackers struck from both sides, creating the illusion of a far larger force. Stone fences and clusters of trees offered immediate cover, turning the terrain into firing positions.

Men crouched behind split-rail fences, weapons loaded, waiting for British troops to enter their sights.

The British, used to disciplined formations, struggled to counter these unpredictable threats. Officers on horseback ordered bayonet charges into brush or volley fire into smoky thickets, while grenadiers pushed through choke points to disperse ambushers. These methods, intended to drive off attackers and clear the road, often forced the British into unfamiliar terrain, where colonial fighters faded away and regrouped elsewhere. At every point, the redcoats found themselves firing blindly or pursuing an enemy always disappearing into the landscape.

Communication faltered for both sides. Militiamen coordinated with runners, hat signals, or horn blasts, but confusion was common. Sometimes, different town companies arrived at the same site and accidentally fired on each other before identifying themselves by town or raised hats—an early and sobering lesson in the fog of war. British lines stretched too thin for orders to carry; messengers weaved through chaos, but gunfire drowned out instructions. The British often overestimated the militia's numbers, heightening the sense of being surrounded.

A pivotal moment came when Captain Parker's Lexington men, after suffering losses at dawn, rejoined the fight later that morning at a wooded rise called Parker's Revenge. Waiting for a vulnerable segment of the redcoat column, they delivered a surprise volley from behind trees and boulders, then disappeared before a counterattack reached them. Their ambush shook the British and boosted colonial spirits.

At "Foot of the Rocks," individual courage shaped events. Militiamen from Cambridge and Menotomy, acting as flanking parties, seized the advantage at a rocky dip in the road. Dashing under fire to secure positions behind stone fences, these men—including a shoemaker in his apron and an old farmer fresh from his plow—blocked a British escape and triggered a fierce musket exchange. Eyewitnesses later described colonials moving quickly from shadow to shadow.

The running battle became a test of adaptability and nerve. Colonial leaders quickly learned to use each rise or thicket to their advantage. The British countered with volleys and bayonet charges but risked new ambushes around each bend. Both sides struggled with confusion—colonials sometimes fired on each other in error; British soldiers rushed past open fields only to face prepared traps.

Success that day depended not on holding ground but on adapting to relentless change. Every carefully planned maneuver collided with improvisation—British officers might shout textbook orders, but colonial farmers acted on instinct behind the nearest hedge. Miscommunication and chaos abounded, but courage and quick thinking often determined the outcome.

Today, walking Battle Road, you can still see the bends and walls where quick decisions and local knowledge gave ordinary people the upper hand. Each field witnessed choices made in seconds but remembered for generations: a captain urging one last volley, a grenadier charging through smoke, a farmer risking everything for a cause still unformed but deeply felt. These moments shaped the course of history, where home-field advantage, swift tactics, and courage under pressure carried the day.

Arrival at Charlestown – Exhaustion, Losses, and British Survival

After relentless fighting and a chaotic retreat, the battered British column finally staggered into Charlestown. The last miles became a test of sheer endurance—many redcoats, uniforms filthy and torn, could scarcely stay upright. Some collapsed from wounds or exhaustion, while others leaned on comrades, dragging themselves onward. Where confident voices had barked orders that morning, now only hoarse whispers and desperate pleas for water remained. The path behind them was marked by the dead and wounded, haunting every survivor.

Casualties mounted steadily as the day dragged on. Men fell to gunfire and bayonet; some were lost or missing in the confusion. Officers who had started the day assured were visibly shaken, their faces etched with fatigue and the realization of how close they came to disaster. The emotional toll was heavy—young soldiers wept, stunned by pain and the shock of their first true battle, shattering illusions of military glory.

Relief finally arrived with General Percy and his fresh brigade near Charlestown Neck. Percy's disciplined, tidy regulars were a stark contrast to the retreating and exhausted men. They quickly set up strong defenses around Charlestown and placed cannon to cover all approaches. The retreating British poured through the lines, finally shielded by bayonets and artillery. Percy wasted no time, establishing a stronghold on the heights and preparing for another colonial attack. For the first time all day, the redcoats could breathe without fear of sudden ambush. Stretcher-bearers aided the wounded, and surgeons tended to the fallen in the dimming light.

But even here, rest was elusive. Colonial militia pressed close to Charlestown's edge, unwilling to let the enemy escape unscathed. Sporadic shots echoed near Prospect Hill and Bunker Hill as militiamen harassed the perimeter, while British artillery thundered back, warning against a direct assault. As dusk fell, colonial leaders recognized further attack meant only more bloodshed. Gradually, the militia withdrew, gathering their wounded and tallying their own losses.

The aftermath brought deep exhaustion and grief on both sides. Makeshift hospitals in Charlestown overflowed with wounded; surgeons worked by candlelight, amputating limbs and saving what lives they could. Colonists, tending to their injured in homes and barns, searched for neighbors who had not returned. Casualty lists grew through the night—names read in sorrowful homes, new graves dug hurriedly in village churchyards.

Survivors' letters—British and colonial alike—capture these raw hours in ways no official report could. British officers confessed fear and confusion to family in England, recounting horrors unimaginable days before. Militiamen wrote of pride and profound loss, struggling to explain a costly victory. In towns from Concord to Boston, stunned silence hung heavy as the news spread, families mourned, and children questioned why their world had changed so suddenly.

The psychological toll was immense. Men who had marched out as farmers and tradesmen returned as changed veterans, scarred by violence they had never wanted to see. Bonds formed among survivors, but new wounds—physical and invisible—would not easily heal. All recognized that April 19th was an ending: there could be no return to former routines.

The day's fighting did more than spill blood. It dismantled illusions—British soldiers saw colonial resistance would not disappear at the first show of force, and colonists learned they could stand against regulars and survive. On April 19th, the old order fractured; uncertainty took hold, but so did determination.

As the moon rose over Charlestown and silence replaced gunfire, survivors understood one thing: the struggle was far from finished. Massachusetts—and soon all the colonies—would face new challenges: building defenses, caring for the wounded in body and spirit, and preparing for a conflict that now seemed both inevitable and unending.

The retreat to Charlestown ended one chapter and began another. Losses weighed heavily on both armies and families. Yet, in exhaustion and grief, resolve took root— independence was no longer distant but a living promise. Ahead lay the tasks of rebuilding, remembering April 19th, and shaping how its echoes would resonate far beyond Massachusetts.

Chapter 7: Aftermath and Echoes Repercussions in Town and Country

Counting the Cost – Casualties, Damage, and Community Response

When dawn broke after the battle, Lexington, Concord, and the neighboring towns confronted a landscape instantly changed by bloodshed. The priority was to tally the loss of life and injury—each figure representing more than a statistic, but a missing member of the community. On April 19, 1775, the colonial militia lost forty-nine killed, forty-one wounded, and five missing; the British counted seventy-three dead, 174 wounded, and twenty-six missing—a staggering cost (see source 1 in APA list). These numbers, far from abstract, rippled through families and towns. John Parker, Lexington militia captain, fell ill after the conflict and died within months, depriving Lexington of its steadfast leader. Jonas Parker, famous for his resolve, died on the ground where he swore never to retreat. Prince Estabrook, an enslaved militiaman, survived with wounds; his story, recorded in parish registers, was remembered by both Black and white townsfolk. In Concord, Isaac Davis of Acton died at North Bridge, leaving his widow and children to the comfort of mourning neighbors. For the British, too, grief was immediate— names like Lieutenant Hull and Private Hugh Montague were recorded in burials and diaries, their fate described in letters reaching families across the Atlantic.

The land itself bore scars of the violence. Residents surveyed what could be saved and what was lost for good. Houses near the main roads had shattered glass, broken shutters, and walls marked by musket fire. Outbuildings were scorched or wrecked in the search for hidden arms. Livestock were gone—driven off or lost in the chaos. Crops were flattened or burned, leaving bare earth. In Menotomy (now Arlington), records detail homes riddled with bullets, wells polluted, and orchards stripped. Concord's leaders kept careful lists of losses, from looted spoons to ruined wagons. Some families lost all of their sheep, others a prized horse. Some property—a table, a tool—was recovered, but much was gone for good. Town meetings logged claims both small and large: "two feather beds torn," "windowpanes broken," "twelve bushels of rye burned," "spinning wheel destroyed."

The community mobilized immediately. Neighbors gathered within hours to bury the dead—sometimes several in a single grave, marked with little more than a wooden board. The following Sunday, church services overflowed with mourners. Sermons, like Reverend Jonas Clarke's in Lexington, urged strength and perseverance: "Affliction may bow us low, but it does not break us." Town meeting records show quick action. In Concord, funds supported widows and orphans; able-bodied volunteers lent labor to families left without their providers. Residents collected food, clothes, and coins for those most in need. In Lincoln, farmers organized to keep up abandoned chores and tend fields. Children who lost parents found guardians in their neighbors. The community made determined efforts so that no family would be left alone with their loss.

Emotionally, the shock was profound, but it fostered resilience. Diaries from the period oscillate between grief and growing resolve. Abigail Harrington wrote, "The air is thick with grief—yet we will gather ourselves." Another Concord resident shared that "every hour since has been burdened by absence," yet added, "our hearts are steeled now to endure." The first days were filled with sorrow and uncertainty, as news came at all hours and families heard of another loss. Still, shared labor and communal action brought solace. As families wept, they also began rebuilding: mending fences, planting gardens, and restoring some order to daily life.

Reflection Exercise: The Ripple Effect of Loss

Choose a casualty's name—perhaps Jonas Parker or Isaac Davis—and note three ways their absence would have changed their family's life after April 19. What tasks would remain undone? Whose voice would be missing at home or at church? Reflect on how the community's support could help—who might step up, and what new bonds might form out of hardship?

Grief and hardship lingered beyond burial or rebuilding; they became a lasting part of local memory and identity. The shared experience of loss drew people into a closer community, forging ties that peace times could not. Reading these stories and names—whether from official ledgers or family Bibles—offers more than numbers; it reveals the lived cost behind the Revolution's first day of violence.

Women's Stories – Survival, Loss, and Rebuilding

While men gathered muskets, women listened for hoofbeats and braced for chaos. Their roles grew immense the moment shots rang out. Letters written in the weeks after the battles paint vivid pictures of women sheltering children under beds, hushing frightened little ones as musket balls pierced walls. In Concord, Mary Barrett described crouching in a cellar, her hands pressed to her son's mouth to stifle his cries while British soldiers searched above. Ruth Harrington's account of that morning reveals her running between house and barn, gathering family and neighbors as the alarm spread, her mind racing with ways to shield those she loved from harm. Some women hid not only themselves but also valuables—silver spoons tucked beneath hearthstones, powder horns buried deep in gardens—anything to keep their families' futures from being seized by war.

A wave of grief swept through kitchens and parlors as news of death reached home. Widows and mothers faced a new world with empty chairs at the table and children asking when fathers would return. Ruth Harrington, left to raise her children after her husband Jonathan fell at Lexington Green, found herself shouldering farm tasks, trading goods with neighbors, and petitioning local authorities for relief. Town records show her name among those who requested compensation for loss—a process requiring not just paperwork, but repeated visits, testimony, and the patience to wait for uncertain decisions. The survival of her family depended on more than courage; it demanded adaptability. She bartered preserves for cloth, sent older children to work for nearby families, and joined with others to make sure no one in the community starved or fell through the cracks. Other widows—like Abigail Munroe and Sarah Estabrook—filed similar petitions, their appeals often supported by neighbors who vouched for their honesty and need.

The work of rebuilding began even before the gunpowder smell faded. Women organized sewing circles in Lexington, Concord, and nearby towns, gathering each week to patch uniforms, knit stockings, and piece together blankets for the militia. These gatherings did more than produce clothing— they built solidarity and created networks that endured beyond the war. Church basements and kitchens became centers of logistics: here, women pooled donations, sorted foodstuffs, and planned deliveries to families most affected by the fighting. Some coordinated relief efforts through their congregations, persuading ministers to announce needs from the pulpit or to allocate funds from church treasuries for widows and orphans. The record of these early efforts survives in meeting notes—lists of names, items produced, and families helped—a testament to quiet organization and steady resolve.

Yet women did more than react; many shaped events as actors in their own right. Some relayed information vital to

Patriot defenses—not always with dramatic midnight rides but through everyday vigilance. Elizabeth Hartwell of Lincoln is remembered for sending coded messages about British troop movements by hanging laundry in certain patterns or delivering news under the guise of routine errands. Other women hid arms or powder kegs beneath heavy barrels or inside flour bins, risking harsh punishment if discovered. A few even influenced major decisions in their own households: matriarchs like Mary Brooks in Lincoln convened family councils to debate whether sons should join the militia or help protect the homestead. In several cases, these women's authority settled disputes and charted the family's course—sometimes toward resistance, sometimes toward caution.

Less visible but no less powerful was the political influence wielded in kitchens and at firesides. Many women shaped their husbands' and sons' views of the conflict by sharing news, discussing sermons on liberty or loyalty, and interpreting rumors that flooded into town after the battles. Some lobbied for action; others urged restraint. When local committees debated controversial votes—such as how to punish suspected Loyalists or whether to send additional supplies—women's opinions often swayed outcomes behind closed doors.

These stories rarely appear in official accounts or marble monuments, yet without them, the recovery from April 19 would have faltered. Each letter preserved, every petition filed, each gathering of neighbors in a kitchen or at a grave marked a step toward restoration. The strength shown in these moments echoed throughout households for years. Women's actions—sometimes bold, sometimes subtle—wove together survival strategies and a spirit of defiance that shaped not only families but also the future of their towns and the Revolution itself.

Their legacies live on in the fabric of community memory: a quilt passed down with stories stitched into every square, a battered pewter cup whose owner once bartered it for a sack of flour, a faded letter describing that first terrifying night. These tangible remnants speak not only of hardship but also of ingenuity and solidarity. When you visit Lexington or Concord today, you stand on ground made secure not just by musket fire but by care—by hands that held trembling children close, that stitched torn sleeves by candlelight, that filled dinner tables with what little could be spared. Through their actions and choices, women shaped both survival and hope after the smoke cleared and history moved forward.

The Role of Loyalists and Neutral Families After the Battles

After the last musket was fired and the British withdrew to Boston, another struggle began for families whose loyalty did not align with the new Patriot order. If you lived in Massachusetts at that time and your sympathies leaned toward the Crown, daily life changed overnight. Suspicion settled on Loyalist households like an unwanted shadow. Neighbors who had once exchanged seeds or borrowed tools now eyed each other with guarded glances. Some

Loyalists faced open hostility—windows shattered by thrown stones, barns marked with threatening symbols, or fences knocked flat in the night. In some cases, angry crowds gathered outside homes, chanting names or hurling insults. Property confiscation became both a punishment and a warning; officials seized livestock, emptied pantries, and auctioned off furniture to raise funds for the Patriot cause. Minutes from town meetings often listed names of suspected Loyalists and detailed what had been taken: "One feather bed, two cows, three barrels of cider." For some, vandalism escalated into violence, forcing entire families to seek shelter with British troops inside Boston's fortified lines.

Many Loyalists, fearing for their safety, abandoned farms and shops they had built over decades. Some took only what they could carry—silver hidden in bread loaves, family Bibles stuffed into saddlebags—while others slipped away at night, leaving homes to be stripped by neighbors or strangers. Ann Hulton of Brookline described packing her belongings after a mob threatened her brother's life, forced to leave behind a garden she had tended for years. A sense of exile haunted these families. In Boston, they joined hundreds of other refugees in overcrowded quarters, trying to rebuild routines in a city under siege. British officers sometimes offered assistance, but resources were thin and tempers short.

Those who tried to remain neutral—"fence-sitters," as they were called—found themselves in an equally perilous position. Some families simply wanted peace and quiet, hoping war would pass them by. Their diaries reveal efforts to avoid notice: attending both Loyalist and Patriot meetings, offering small donations to both causes, and keeping public opinions vague or masked by polite conversation. A Concord farmer wrote about spending days mending fences while neighbors argued over politics. He recorded changing his meetinghouse seat every Sunday so as not to appear aligned with any particular faction. Minutes from local hearings show that suspicion reached even those who tried to remain invisible; committees called citizens to account for their loyalties. If a person hesitated or offered evasive answers, whispers spread quickly. Sometimes these hearings ended with formal warnings or demands for public declarations of support.

Punishment for Loyalist sympathizers became both official and unofficial. Town mobs sometimes dragged men suspected of aiding the British through the streets, stripping them to the waist and covering them in tar and feathers—a humiliating ordeal intended to leave a mark both literal and figurative. Public shaming did not stop at the town line; news of such punishments traveled fast and wide thanks to broadsides and word of mouth. The Provincial Congress passed laws targeting property owned by those who refused to pledge allegiance to the Provincial cause. Officials could seize possessions or impose fines without much recourse for appeal. Towns sometimes required oaths of loyalty before allowing trade or entry into local markets, making it impossible for Loyalists or neutrals to participate in daily commerce without risking exposure.

The consequences rippled out into every corner of community life. Marriages that once united Patriot and Loyalist families found themselves strained or broken apart by suspicion and anger. Some couples separated rather than live under constant threat; others endured, but at the cost of social isolation. Churches that had welcomed everyone at the same pew began to fracture—congregations split over which prayers should be said for king or colony. Pastors who refused to take sides risked dismissal or worse; some left their pulpits altogether. Business relationships dissolved as merchants on different sides cut ties—credit lines vanished, partnerships ended abruptly, and apprenticeships were canceled without notice.

Migrations reshaped the region's population map. Dozens of families left for Halifax or Nova Scotia, hoping for British protection and a fresh start; others sailed for England, carrying with them only memories and whatever valuables they could smuggle past Patriot patrols. Town records tracked these departures with terse notes: "Gone to Canada," "departed for England," "fled under cover of darkness." Those who remained behind faced years of hardship rebuilding trust—or living with the knowledge that they were now outsiders in their own land.

Yet even among all this turmoil, some found ways to adapt. A few Loyalists quietly returned after tempers cooled, reestablishing their farms on the edges of town or taking up trades in distant communities. Fence-sitters evolved into cautious citizens, learning to read the political winds before speaking out loud. Over time, grudges faded but seldom vanished completely; stories of betrayals or reconciliations lingered in family lore and local gossip for generations. The Revolution's violence had not only divided armies—it had also divided neighborhoods and kin, leaving scars that would take decades to heal but never quite disappear from memory.

News Spreads – Broadsides, Rumors, and the Birth of a Narrative

Almost immediately after the first shots at Lexington and Concord, news swept across New England. In Boston, printers worked overnight to produce broadsides—urgent, ink-fresh sheets packed with eyewitness accounts from militiamen and townsfolk. Stories recounted the chaos, redcoats charging, and muskets firing. Express riders sped these bulletins to New York and beyond, while in Philadelphia, readers devoured reports of courage and confrontation by week's end. News traveled by post roads and ferries, often faster than official couriers. Patriots like printer Isaiah Thomas relocated presses to safer towns and spread news as far as Virginia and South Carolina. Each account amplified the sense of irreversible change.

Alongside printed news, rumors mushroomed and often veered from fact. In taverns and coffeehouses, men swapped tales of entire British regiments destroyed or towns burned. Some said hundreds of colonists were dead, or claimed the British executed prisoners and torched houses. Heroic deeds ballooned with each telling—a boy supplying powder amid gunfire, a grandmother rescuing the wounded. Many stories started with truth, but soon turned into legend. Newspapers fanned these rumors, sometimes inflating casualty numbers and blending action with hearsay. Even cautious voices struggled to restrain exaggeration as tension and excitement gripped the colonies.

Propaganda was wielded as effectively as any musket. Patriot leaders realized the significance of the moment and crafted their messages deliberately. Broadsides starkly divided righteous colonists from invading British oppressors. Letters from Committees of Correspondence warned that the king's men had opened fire on peaceful townsfolk, proclaiming liberty in grave danger. The language was intentionally stirring, meant to rally emotion and conviction. Some broadsides quoted sermons or poetry, framing the colonial cause as divinely supported and condemning British troops as tyrants. These proclamations were read aloud at gatherings or posted in public, making sure the message reached even the illiterate.

This explosion of news had an immediate political effect. Towns held emergency meetings, often within hours of receiving word, to plan their responses. In both rural villages and bustling ports, resolutions were passed supporting the arming of militias and stockpiling of powder. Town clerks issued declarations: We will resist; we are united; we will defend our rights. Volunteer lists quickly filled. Church bells called citizens to meetings, turning religious centers into hubs of wartime organization. The Second Continental Congress convened with delegates armed with stories—some true, some exaggerated—intent on ensuring no colony faced the crisis alone. Debates in Congress intensified, split between calls for reconciliation and demands for resistance and independence.

The shock reached well beyond colonial shores. Merchant ships crossing the Atlantic delivered reports to London, arriving before letters from British officers. Government ministers received these dispatches, and London papers published extracts from colonial broadsides alongside terse official updates from General Gage. The British press responded with disbelief, outrage, and fascination. Some outlets called colonists traitors; others suggested negotiation and even expressed sympathy for "fellow Britons driven to desperation." Parliamentary debates erupted, with heated arguments over who caused the violence—government hardliners or colonial rebels? Members scrutinized casualty lists and firsthand testimonies.

Within days, the British public and officials reacted: merchants worried about lost trade; politicians proposed sending more troops or negotiating. Distance from the colonies only deepened confusion, concern, and a sense of urgency about the war's true costs. The Atlantic did not dampen the impact; if anything, it magnified the stakes.

Infographic: How News Traveled in 1775

- **Broadsides:** Single sheets posted in public, often recopied and widely circulated.

- **Express Riders:** Relayed news rapidly, sometimes covering 100 miles a day.
- **Committees of Correspondence:** Shared news using coded letters and trusted couriers.
- **Newspapers:** Published weekly or semi-weekly, frequently reprinting news from other cities.
- **Merchant Ships:** Carried bundled newspapers and letters to England for quick delivery.
- **Word of Mouth:** News passed by travelers, often changing with each retelling.

The swift spread of news after Lexington and Concord was pivotal—not just as a military event, but in forging a shared American identity. The story outgrew two towns, capturing an entire continent's imagination—and soon, the world's.

The Mythmaking Begins – Paul Revere, the First Shot, and National Memory

From the moment the fighting at Lexington and Concord ended, people began shaping the story into more than a local event. Paul Revere's name quickly spread, but not always accurately. In his original deposition, taken days after the battle, Revere described passing quietly through the countryside as part of a network warning leaders like Samuel Adams and John Hancock. He did not present himself as a lone hero, but as just one among several riders raising the alarm. Yet, over time, his role was recast in popular memory: the quiet relay of warnings turned into a dramatic, singular ride, his supposed warning—"The British are coming!"—replacing what he and others actually said: "The regulars are out," reflecting that most people still considered themselves British.

With each anniversary and retelling, the mythmaking accelerated. Local leaders realized early on that the meaning of the battles would outlast the violence. Both Samuel Adams and John Hancock, who were in Lexington on April 19, focused on commemorating the event. Through speeches, correspondence, and organized remembrances, they helped shape the first public narratives, emphasizing unity and sacrifice and framing the conflict as an ordinary people's fight for liberty. Their accounts became the foundation for political speeches and newspapers, and the first annual gatherings on Lexington Green served not only locals but also marked the beginning of a national story of American birth.

Writers and teachers soon added their own embellishments. Ralph Waldo Emerson, nearly sixty years later, immortalized the conflict with "Concord Hymn" and its famous phrase, "the shot heard 'round the world." Written for a monument dedication at North Bridge, the poem soon featured in textbooks and public events across the country. Emerson's words condensed a chaotic, confusing day into a powerful moment of destiny, one that students memorized and teachers used to teach patriotism. The phrase became a fixture in American education, politics, and memory.

However, the true history was less dramatic. Careful reading of Revere's own words—his deposition, letters—shows a story of cooperation: rides coordinated with

William Dawes and Samuel Prescott, arrests by British patrols, and help from many others along the route. Modern historians have contrasted these firsthand accounts with Henry Wadsworth Longfellow's 1860 poem "Paul Revere's Ride," which transformed Revere into a lone hero thundering through the night, turning a collective warning into an individual act of heroism. Longfellow's version matched a 19th-century appetite for national heroes but departed from the facts.

For years, schoolbooks spread these myths. They described Revere riding alone, shouting the now-iconic "The British are coming," and depicted a single, world-changing shot at dawn. Physical memorials reinforced these versions, with monuments and plaques quoting lines from poems and speeches rather than from those who were actually present. "The shot heard 'round the world" became a shorthand for the Revolution's beginning, repeated in classrooms, parades, and campaigns.

Those shaping the myths did so consciously. Samuel Adams wrote resolutions framing the conflict as a fight for universal rights, and John Hancock sent impassioned letters to unite the colonies. Ceremonies combined fact with ideals, focusing on larger themes of shared purpose rather than confusing battlefield details. Physical memorials gave the stories staying power, rooting memory in both geography and public imagination.

Today, historians work to untangle fact from legend, using sidebars and original documents. Comparing Revere's own accounts to Longfellow's poem and later textbooks, stark differences appear: "regulars" changed to "British"; a network of riders became one "midnight rider"; a clear, theatrical warning replaced more measured alarms. These differences show how national memory is shaped as much by desires and identity as by actual history.

The mythmaking did not stop in the nineteenth century. School curricula through the twentieth century continued to recite the legend of Paul Revere and Emerson's poetic line, making them pillars of American self-image. Textbooks often left out Dawes and Prescott, and reenactments further embedded these stories in local and national tradition.

Ultimately, these myths did more than keep events alive— they defined American identity. The tale of a midnight rider and a single shot became enduring symbols of courage and unity. Studying the evolution of these stories gives insight not only into Lexington and Concord, but also into how nations remember and commemorate their beginnings.

Mourning and Memorials – How Lexington and Concord Remember

In the days after the battles, mourning took form through shared rituals and quiet gestures. On Lexington Green, Concord's burying ground, and in small family plots, communities gathered for the first communal burials. These ceremonies, marked by the tolling of bells and the hush of neighbors pressed together in grief, provided an anchor for sorrow and remembrance. Fresh earth covered newly dug graves, while ministers read prayers and family members wept. The names of the fallen echoed in prayers and sermons, spoken aloud so that even those too young to remember would come to know the weight of sacrifice. The following spring, as April returned, towns marked the anniversary with special church services and processions. Such gatherings became an annual rhythm—neighbors walking together from the meetinghouse to the green, pausing where blood had once stained the grass, then returning home with heavy hearts but a sense of unity.

As the years passed, these acts of memory took on a physical presence. The people of Lexington and Concord erected stone markers at burial sites, first as simple headstones carved with names and dates. By the early nineteenth century, more formal monuments began to rise. The Lexington Battle Green Monument stands as a granite sentinel, its inscription a public vow to remember those who died "in the cause of Liberty." In Concord, at North Bridge, another memorial took shape—a granite obelisk that names the first to fall in open resistance to British arms. These sites were not built in haste; decades of debate shaped their design and placement. Each plaque, each monument, reflects choices about what to honor and who to include. Over time, private homes where key moments unfolded— Buckman Tavern in Lexington, the Old Manse by North Bridge—were preserved and opened to visitors. The landscape itself became a living memorial, dotted with signs and stones that invite reflection as you walk the paths trodden by those long gone.

Commemoration evolved beyond local rituals into wider traditions as Massachusetts—and eventually the United States—sought to make meaning from the past. Patriots' Day emerged as an official holiday in the late nineteenth century, first celebrated in Massachusetts before spreading to other states. This day did not merely recall old battles; it became a time for parades, speeches, and reenactments that brought history alive for new generations. Each April, schoolchildren dressed as militia marked out the lines on Lexington Green, while men and women in period garb fired salutes at North Bridge. Minute Man National Historical Park grew from these traditions, preserving fields and trails so that visitors could encounter history firsthand. Historic tourism flourished—families from across the country traveled to see where "the shot heard 'round the world" rang out. Local guides told stories passed down through generations, blending fact with legend yet always returning to the theme of sacrifice for a greater good.

Memory does not stand still. With each generation, debates over how to remember Lexington and Concord have surfaced. Some argue over the accuracy of plaques or displays—was this house really where a key meeting took place? Did this stone mark the exact spot of the first shot? Local historians sift through records and testimonies, sometimes revising old narratives or adding context. In recent decades, efforts have grown to include voices long overlooked: Black soldiers like Prince Estabrook now have their stories told alongside others, while Indigenous perspectives begin to appear in exhibits and ceremonies.

New plaques name women who risked much on April 19 or cared for the wounded in its aftermath. Community groups push for more inclusive commemorations—recognizing not only those who fought but also those who struggled for belonging or justice in a divided land.

These shifts invite questions about who gets remembered and how. Some traditions endure: processions across Lexington Green at dawn, wreath-laying at North Bridge, quiet moments in shaded graveyards where names worn by weather still speak volumes. Other practices change as new residents bring fresh perspectives or as scholarship uncovers forgotten chapters. The conversation over memory remains alive—a sign not of confusion but of a community's commitment to truth and meaning.

Through all these rituals—solemn burials, annual processions, monuments rising against sky and stone—Lexington and Concord have become more than places on a map. They are sites where memory is made and remade, where each generation faces the past and decides how best to honor it. These commemorations do not erase pain or resolve every debate, but they bind communities across time. They offer you a way to connect with loss and courage from centuries ago—to walk among stones that witnessed history and to carry forward lessons shaped by grief and hope.

In closing this chapter, you see how remembrance shapes not only what is recalled but also who belongs to the story. Mourning gives way to memory; monuments prompt questions as well as pride. These practices ensure that April 19 never fades into silence but continues to echo—inviting you to reflect on sacrifice, belonging, and the meaning of freedom as you look ahead to what followed after those first shots of revolution.

Chapter 8: Legacies and Landmarks
Walking the Route Today

Walking the Battle Road – A Step-by-Step Guide for Today's Visitors

Picture yourself at the edge of a winding trail, sunlight filtering through the trees, and the sounds of both nature and distant modern life in the air. Beneath your feet runs the Battle Road Trail—a five-mile path from Lexington to Concord. Nearly 250 years ago, this was a route of fear, news, and resolve, echoing with boots and musket fire. Today, it invites visitors to connect with a living landscape steeped in the events of April 19, 1775.

Begin your walk at Lexington Green, open year-round, and the place where the Revolutionary War began. Here, visualize Captain Parker's militia at dawn, townspeople filled with uncertainty, and British regulars advancing. A nearby monument honors the locals who fell; pause here to reflect on how regular people can be thrust into extraordinary circumstances.

From Lexington Green, head northwest along Massachusetts Avenue to the well-marked Battle Road Trail. The mostly level trail winds through meadows, woods, and farmland—ideal for families, with interpretive signs for context. Two miles in, you'll reach Meriam's Corner, where militia from surrounding towns joined the fight as the British retreated. A stone marker and narrative signage commemorate this pivotal moment—pause here to consider how a joint effort turned the tide.

Continue to Bloody Angle, a sharp curve shaded by trees and enclosed by New England stone walls. This site saw particularly fierce combat, as colonists used every thicket and bend for cover. Imagine the confusion and tension as you walk among the terrain; prompts or sketches can help visitors, especially students, put themselves into that morning.

Further west is Hartwell Tavern, a restored 18th-century building and notable waystation on April 19th. The surrounding area is open with picnic spots and rest stops—on special days, you may encounter reenactors or park rangers. Take the opportunity to ask about tactics or daily life in 1775.

Continue west toward the North Bridge in Concord, the site of the "shot heard 'round the world." Though reconstructed, the bridge stands at the original river crossing. Read the interpretive signage and think about how geography—rivers, woods, fields—influenced both colonial and British decisions and strategies.

Minute Man National Historical Park supports navigation with an interactive mobile app featuring detailed maps, audio guides, primary sources, and AR content (Source 1). QR codes at major sites deliver eyewitness accounts and video to your smartphone. Paper maps, free at visitor centers on Route 2A, also highlight stops and amenities.

Choosing when to visit can reshape your experience. Spring is lively, with wildflowers, cool breezes, and Patriots' Day reenactments, though crowds are common. Fall brings beautiful foliage and quieter paths. Summer is popular, though the trail may be muddy after rain, so sturdy shoes are recommended.

Most of the Battle Road Trail has packed gravel paths accessible to wheelchairs and strollers, with clearly marked ADA-accessible parking (notably at Meriam's Corner and Hartwell Tavern, Source 1). Restrooms are available near visitor centers, and benches throughout offer rest and reflection spots.

To further enrich your visit, join a ranger-led tour or attend living history programs during Patriots' Day week each April. These events feature musket demonstrations, tactical drills, and engaging narratives. Activities for kids include booklets and scavenger hunts via mobile devices; adults may enjoy immersive audio tours using historic letters and expert commentary.

Historic Homes, Taverns, and the People Who Lived There

Walking along the route of April 19th, you retrace the steps not only of soldiers but also of ordinary people caught in extraordinary times. At the heart of Lexington stands Buckman Tavern, a silent witness to history. Its thick beams, uneven floors, and period features—broad hearth, hand-forged latches, and central taproom—remain as they were in 1775. Here, Captain Parker's militia gathered, some young and anxious, others weathered by experience. Look closely at the old wood to see faint eighteenth-century graffiti—initials carved by men awaiting battle. Buckman Tavern isn't sealed off behind glass; it welcomes visitors for guided tours from spring through fall. Costumed interpreters recount stories of strategy, alarm, and the careful hiding of powder and shot under floorboards, immersing guests in the moment's tension.

Further west, Munroe Tavern tells a different story. On April 19th, the Munroe family saw their home seized and transformed into a field hospital for British wounded. The kitchen was commandeered; the injured lay on beds and tables, blood staining the floorboards while musket balls became lodged in the walls. Now a museum, Munroe Tavern allows visitors to stand in the family's dining room and hear tales of Anna Munroe tending to wounded strangers and protecting her children amid chaos. The blackened fireplace remains a storytelling focal point. Guides sometimes reveal a hidden pantry nook where valuables were stashed—a physical reminder of how quickly daily life could change.

Hartwell Tavern in Lincoln adds another layer. Built in the 1730s, it has survived war and weather with its sturdy clapboards and narrow stairways. On April 19th, Ephraim Hartwell watched the British column pass by, and his home became a relay point for alarm riders heading to Concord. Family members prepared provisions and bandages, listening for news. Today, living history interpreters demonstrate colonial crafts, fire flintlock muskets, and share how one family's home became a hub of hope and fear. Children try colonial games; adults appreciate the preserved kitchen garden and barroom ceiling beams. Ask a guide, and you might see a concealed cupboard behind the hearth, used to hide powder or documents—a detail easy to overlook.

The Jason Russell House in Arlington stands out for its tragedy. On April 19th, Russell, refusing to flee, prepared his house for defense and hid valuables. When fleeing militia entered, British soldiers broke in after a skirmish; Russell was killed at his doorstep with others. Bloodstains lingered on the floorboards for decades. Today, the house preserves its original floors, bullet holes, and narrow staircases. Local historians lead tours that recount not just the day's violence but also family life—meals interrupted by alarms, children hiding, neighbors rallying. Hours vary, admission is modest, and docents eagerly discuss both routines and architectural quirks, like staircases built for warmth, or secret crawlspaces.

Each site offers more than a static display—they invite tactile, immersive experiences. In Buckman and Munroe Taverns, expect hands-on exhibits: handle reproduction powder horns or try colonial handwriting with a quill. Hartwell Tavern often features open-hearth cooking and militia drills, bringing to life both the urgency and routine of 1775. Jason Russell House hosts programs such as candlelit tours and storytelling sessions, echoing voices from the past.

Some "insider" details add depth: Buckman Tavern's taproom displays initials carved by men awaiting news from Revere or Dawes, like a living autograph book. Munroe Tavern's pantry still shows marks from hastily hidden valuables. Hartwell Tavern's attic hides an original powder closet for both supplies and family secrets. The Jason Russell House has a back staircase with uneven risers, a practical architectural quirk explained by guides.

These buildings are not relics frozen in time, but bridges to the past—places where questions of courage, loss, hope, and survival are revisited by each visitor who steps across their thresholds.

Minute Man National Historical Park – Interpreting the Landscape

Minute Man National Historical Park stretches across the old fields, forests, and lanes where the first day of the Revolution unfolded. Its mission is both clear and ambitious: to preserve the physical legacy of April 19, 1775, while also making the stories of those hours understandable and meaningful for you today. The park was established in the late 1950s, a time when highways and new housing threatened to erase many original landscapes. Local citizens, historians, teachers, and preservationists worked together, raising their voices to make sure the ground where the Revolution began would not be lost to bulldozers or neglect. Their advocacy paid off. Congress created Minute Man National Historical Park in 1959, protecting not just famous landmarks but also the meadows, stone walls, and even some of the "witness houses" where civilians watched history unfold (Source 2).

The park's design reflects this commitment to authenticity and access. Instead of isolating visitors from the landscape, its trails wind right through meadows and groves much as they did two centuries ago. Modern roads run parallel but never overwhelm; you can walk or roll along wide gravel paths where militia once marched. Interpretive philosophy here means you are encouraged to see, touch, and contemplate—not just observe behind velvet ropes. Park staff work closely with local communities, consulting town historians and descendants whose families have lived here for generations. Their input shapes everything from trail restoration to new exhibits, keeping interpretation rooted in both scholarship and lived memory.

Two visitor centers anchor the park experience. The North Bridge Visitor Center in Concord sits on a rise overlooking the famous river crossing. Inside, you'll find multimedia exhibits—paintings, artifacts, interactive maps—designed to bring both the battle and its aftermath to life. Orientation films play throughout the day, blending eyewitness accounts with re-enacted scenes and expert commentary. Just off Route 2A stands the Battle Road Visitor Center, a gateway for those exploring the main trail. Here you encounter dynamic displays using soundscapes, digital timelines, and primary source quotations; the result is a sense of immediacy, placing you in the midst of decisions faced by both soldiers and civilians.

Interpretive signage is never an afterthought. Along every trail and at each crossroads, you'll see carefully placed panels with maps, period images, and historical context. Many signs include quotations from diaries or letters so that the voices of 1775 are never far away. You might read a line from Captain John Parker or a local woman whose home stood nearby. These signs help you connect each physical location with the choices and emotions of that day.

Education is at the heart of everything here. School groups visit throughout the year—sometimes filling the air with excited questions as they follow costumed guides over the greens. Teachers have access to downloadable lesson plans crafted by park educators, which align with state standards but also invite students to wrestle with big questions about liberty and justice. Workshops for teachers provide resources for classroom use and strategies for making primary sources come alive. The Junior Ranger program offers children an activity booklet filled with puzzles, scavenger hunts, and sketching prompts; after completion, rangers award badges during a short pledge ceremony that echoes themes of citizenship and stewardship.

Park interpreters lead guided walks daily in peak season, offering insight into tactics, civilian life, and ecology. Whether you join a ranger at North Bridge for a tactical demonstration or walk Battle Road with an educator discussing women's roles in 1775, you'll find each experience crafted for clarity and engagement. Special programs—like "History at Sunset" or "Patriots' Day

Muster"—draw locals and travelers alike, making history feel both immediate and participatory.

Ongoing research keeps discovery alive here. Recent archaeological digs at sites such as Parker's Revenge have changed our understanding of how militia maneuvered and where bodies may have fallen on April 19th. Archaeologists use ground-penetrating radar, careful mapping, and even soil analysis to locate musket balls or remnants of earthworks. These projects sometimes uncover artifacts—a coat button, a musket flint—that are then displayed in the visitor centers with updated interpretive panels explaining their significance. Restoration work also extends to stone walls, historic fields, and wetlands; landscape architects reference period maps, letters, and paintings to guide every planting or wall repair.

Conservation is ongoing as well. The park works to maintain 18th-century viewsheds by removing invasive species and planting trees native to colonial Massachusetts. Stone walls are rebuilt by hand using traditional methods; meadows are mowed on a schedule that mimics colonial farming rhythms. Each project aims to balance historical accuracy with modern needs for accessibility and sustainability.

Minute Man National Historical Park is not just a memorial but a living classroom—a place where preservation meets storytelling, where you can stand in the footsteps of those who made history and see how their choices shaped not only a nation but also the contours of your own life today.

Artifacts and Relics – What Survives from April 1775?

When you step into a gallery lined with relics from the battles of Lexington and Concord, you physically connect with the narrative in a way that words alone cannot match. Among the rarest and most powerful objects is the musket widely attributed to Captain John Parker, commander of the Lexington militia. Its walnut stock, worn smooth in places by decades of handling, tells its own story—modern experts have traced its history through Parker's family, local inventories, and restoration records. Spotting the initials "JP" faintly carved near the trigger guard, you realize this was more than a weapon; it was an extension of Parker's own resolve on the morning he gave his famous order to stand firm. The musket now rests in a climate-controlled case at the Lexington Historical Society, where staff are eager to explain its provenance and significance, drawing on depositions and family lore.

Another artifact that draws attention is a British grenadier's mitre cap, recovered in the fields near Meriam's Corner. Its faded red cloth and tarnished brass badge carry the scars of battle and time. This particular cap surfaced during late nineteenth-century plowing, unearthed by a Concord farmer who recognized its foreign design from old prints and immediately notified local historians. Subsequent research connected it to a regiment listed in British muster rolls present on April 19, 1775. The Concord Museum now displays it as part of a Revolutionary War gallery, pairing it with musket balls, bayonets, and other material evidence from the day. Standing before this cap, you sense the presence of an individual British soldier—one who never reclaimed his lost headgear as the battle's chaos swept him away.

The path from battlefield relic to museum exhibit is rarely straightforward. Many artifacts owe their survival to happenstance or persistent community effort. Take, for example, the musket balls excavated at North Bridge during the 1800s. Locals scouring the banks after spring floods spotted small lead spheres, some flattened or deeply gouged. Early collectors preserved these finds as souvenirs, labeling each one with location and, sometimes, date of discovery. Over time, these collections became scattered among private hands, historical societies, and university holdings. Occasionally, rumors of "lost" or stolen artifacts spark heated debate—stories circulate of powder horns or uniform buttons disappearing from attics or being spirited away by unscrupulous dealers. Museums today rely on careful documentation and forensic analysis to authenticate what they display.

Community and family heirlooms add another dimension to the story of preservation. The Harrington family's powder horn, for instance, traveled through five generations before reaching public view. Its scrimshawed surface features not only geometric patterns but also an inscription: "Lexington April 19th." This piece was hidden in an attic trunk for decades before descendants realized its larger significance. Now, exhibited at the Lexington Historical Society, it stands as both a family treasure and a national relic. Diaries written by townspeople provide equally valuable links; handwritten entries describe alarm bells ringing at midnight or recount the shock of seeing wounded neighbors brought home. Some diaries have remained within families for centuries, passed down as sacred texts, while others surfaced in estate sales or archival donations.

The process of recovering and authenticating these relics is meticulous. Museum curators consult old town inventories, probate records, and even photographs taken in the earliest days of American preservation efforts. Forensic specialists analyze wood grain on muskets or fabric weave in uniforms to confirm authenticity. Occasionally, contested claims arise—a powder horn with an ambiguous inscription or a musket missing clear provenance will spark scholarly debate, complete with published articles and expert panels.

You can view many of these artifacts firsthand at local institutions. The Concord Museum's Revolutionary War gallery houses dozens of period objects—alongside the mitre cap, there are British cartridge boxes, fragments of military gear, and civilian items like shoe buckles or clay pipes found near battle sites. Multimedia displays pair objects with maps and contemporary accounts, creating an immersive learning experience. The Lexington Historical Society maintains rotating exhibits that feature battle-damaged doors, militia drums, and family letters describing April 19th as it unfolded.

Personal relics—letters penned by wives to absent husbands, fragments of clothing worn into battle, or even children's toys found near witness houses—continue to surface across the region. Each object acts as a mnemonic device, evoking details that might otherwise fade from collective memory. Family members still bring items forward for assessment: a powder flask tucked inside a chest for generations or a bundle of yellowed papers tied with ribbon found behind a false wall.

These physical reminders make history tangible. They connect you not only to famous names but also to countless anonymous men and women whose choices shaped what followed. As you examine these artifacts—whether in glass cases or family albums—you become part of an ongoing story: one where discovery, preservation, and interpretation ensure that April 1775 will always be more than just words on a page.

Community Voices – Descendants, Reenactors, and Local Historians

For many local families, the events of April 19, 1775, still resonate as personal history. Descendants of those present on Lexington Green or nearby homes continue to share stories of their ancestors—stories passed through generations. One notable thread is from Prince Estabrook's descendants. Estabrook, an enslaved man wounded at Lexington, is remembered by his family for both his bravery and the ongoing struggle for freedom after the battle. Family members describe tracing his name on muster rolls and visiting his grave each spring, with elders recounting how his injury brought both pride and sorrow. For them, April 19th is not just history; it's a vital part of family identity, with themes of resilience and dignity.

Other families, like the Parkers and Munroes, maintain similarly powerful connections. A Parker descendant remembers hearing stories as a child about Captain John Parker's famous order, "Stand your ground." These words have become family touchstones, symbolizing courage in the face of adversity. The Munroes still recount tales of their ancestors' tavern serving as a field hospital and the ensuing chaos—memories filled with stories of hidden valuables, strangers, and uncertain hours after the British left. Such family lore is not fixed but evolves with each generation, adapting as new information and perspectives emerge.

Modern reenactors have also become keepers of this history. Groups like the Lexington Minute Men and local British "Redcoats" dedicate themselves to detailed research and preparation for annual Patriots' Day events. They spend months studying period letters, drilling with muskets, and perfecting uniforms to historical accuracy. Standing on Lexington Green before dawn in April, they speak of the adrenaline and anxiety reminiscent of that historic morning. For them, authenticity involves more than costumes; it's about inhabiting the mindsets of those from 1775, debating tactics, practicing era-specific speech, and imagining the uncertainty of the original participants. After reenactments, they often engage with visitors, sometimes staying in character, creating a bridge to the past.

Patriots' Day events go beyond ceremonies for these reenactors. Many feel a deep responsibility to honor those who came before and to share stories faithfully. They note that moments of quiet—between musket volleys or as dawn light covers the monuments—are when history's weight is most felt. New research or different social conversations sometimes prompt revisions to their presentations, including changes in scripts or costumes to better reflect the diversity present in 1775.

Local historians, educators, and park rangers act as the stewards of both memory and evidence. Oral history projects, sometimes led by staff at the Minute Man National Historical Park, have collected interviews with older residents whose relatives remembered earlier centennials or maintained family relics. Historians balance accuracy with accessibility and strive to separate myth from fact, often expanding the narrative to include previously excluded voices—such as Loyalist families who left for Canada, women who offered post-battle relief, or children who retained fragmented memories throughout their lives.

Interpretations of the past are continually developing. Community groups actively work to include stories once overlooked. At Concord's Robbins House, interpreters highlight African American history, displaying exhibits about the area's formerly enslaved and free Black residents who influenced local society before and after the Revolution. Visitors can read first-person letters from Black Concordians and learn about abolitionists whose activism was inspired by Revolutionary values. Park programs now also feature Indigenous narratives, incorporating Narragansett and Nipmuc perspectives and setting April 19th within the wider span of Native history in the area.

Educators and local activists add to this narrative tapestry. School projects might pair students with elders to record memories, or ask families to loan documents for special exhibits. Women's organizations research the diaries and letters of wives, mothers, and daughters who stirred community efforts or negotiated during times of upheaval.

By weaving together family memory, reenactments, archival research, and activism, the meaning of Lexington and Concord continues to expand. Each new voice or project brings nuance; participants become both learners and storytellers. The memory of April 1775 is kept alive not just in official records, but in kitchens, classrooms, parades, and community meetings—where all involved are invited to remember, question, and contribute.

Myths, Memory, and the Enduring Meaning of April 19, 1775

Over two centuries, the story of Lexington and Concord has grown beyond what happened on that single day. As eyewitnesses faded, later generations, needing symbols and unifying moments, crafted legends and filled gaps with their own ideals. "The shot heard 'round the world," for instance, became a national touchstone not for its historical accuracy, but for its power as a founding myth. Longfellow's famous poem, while stirring, simplifies the complicated system of alarm riders into the actions of a single heroic figure. This blending of fact and legend isn't unique—every nation shapes its identity with both.

National anniversaries, like the 1875 centennial, have been key in shaping how these events are remembered. Monument dedications, parades, and speeches often merged history with patriotic feeling, turning places like Lexington Green and North Bridge into powerful sites for civic reflection. As America changed—facing wars, social changes, and shifting ideas of freedom—commemorations evolved too. Focus shifted from military tactics to broader questions: Who is included in these stories? Whose sacrifices do we acknowledge? In classrooms, "the shot heard 'round the world'" now symbolizes both revolution and possibility, while the messy reality of that day is often glossed over in favor of simplified narratives and boldface names.

Patriots' Day traditions continue to keep these memories fresh. Parades and reenactments link past and present for many, but their meaning has shifted. Once focused on colonial fighters, these events now also highlight women who nursed the wounded, Black militiamen like Prince Estabrook, and Loyalist families. These additions reflect a growing desire to include more voices in the nation's founding narrative.

Remembering, however, is never impartial. Every act of commemoration—the selection of monuments, plaques, and public art—involves choices about what to celebrate and who to leave out. In recent decades, debates have increased over which stories are told. Some argue that existing monuments ignore certain perspectives, especially those of Black and Indigenous participants, leading to new plaques, exhibits, and sometimes heated public meetings about what to add or change. This evolving dialogue is important, as it shapes how future generations understand the Revolution and their own identities.

Expanding historical memory isn't just about adding names—it asks us to challenge simple stories and see the complexities of the past. For example, Black soldiers fighting for promises of liberty highlight both hope and contradiction, while Native experiences reveal losses and alliances that complicate tales of heroism. Broadening the story helps deepen our understanding of April 19 and its wider impact then and now.

Everyone has a part to play in shaping history's legacy. Local historical societies and parks invite public involvement, from volunteering for research and artifact curation to leading tours or organizing events. Families with letters, diaries, or heirlooms from April 19th can enrich museums or archives by sharing their stories. Every contribution adds to the shared record.

Active engagement also means asking who is missing from public memorials, how we recognize both bravery and conflict, and whether we honor women's, Black, and Indigenous contributions. Supporting projects that enrich the story fosters a more complete history. Even simple discussions with students or at home keep history relevant and alive.

The way Lexington and Concord are remembered reveals not just the past, but also our current values surrounding identity and belonging. Each generation revisits April 19th through its own lens. Myths can unify or exclude; our challenge is to use memory for deeper understanding rather than division.

In conclusion, every retelling—whether in textbooks, parades, or private conversations—shapes what April 19 means to you and your community. The legacy is alive in every debate, lesson, and commemoration. Lexington and Concord endure not just as locations, but as symbols of how ordinary people can shape historic change—and how we, too, can help keep those stories meaningful for generations to come.

Next, we'll see how these lessons resonate far beyond Massachusetts, influencing ongoing national conversations about freedom, citizenship, and American identity.

Conclusion

History's hinge often turns on moments so brief, so fraught with confusion, that even those who stood in the thick of it could not say with certainty what had passed or what it meant. The morning of April 19, 1775—when the first shots cracked across the dew-damp green of Lexington and echoed at Concord's North Bridge—was such a moment. In those few tense hours, the American Revolution leapt from words to action. The path from protest to independence, once unthinkable, suddenly became the new reality. The world changed, not with grand speeches or declarations, but with the choices of ordinary people facing extraordinary pressure. This, above all, is the truth at the heart of Lexington and Concord.

Throughout this book, I have invited you to walk that road with me—from the first uneasy whispers in Massachusetts town squares to the thunder of muskets, and on through the long shadow that day cast over families, fields, and future generations. We traced the mounting tension, as taxes and Parliament's decrees tested the patience and unity of colonial communities. We followed the alarm riders—Paul Revere, William Dawes, Samuel Prescott, and dozens more—who risked the darkness and British patrols to spread the warning. Together, we stood on the green at Lexington and the bridge at Concord, watching as split-second decisions and frayed nerves tipped a continent into open conflict. We marched the harrowing road back to

Boston, saw the countryside rise up in fury, and stepped inside homes shattered by violence.

This journey has uncovered lasting insights, and I urge you to carry them forward. The question of who fired the first shot—so often framed as a simple matter—remains a tangle of testimony, confusion, and fear. No single witness could see the whole field, and each account reflects the teller's hopes, loyalties, and anxieties. This ambiguity is no flaw; it is the mark of history lived, not manufactured. What is clear is the courage shown on all sides—by militiamen holding their ground, by British soldiers thrust into a hostile landscape, by women shielding their children and hiding supplies, by Black and Indigenous men who risked their lives for a cause still defining itself. Communication and intelligence—by alarm riders, spies, and committees— proved as decisive as any musket or bayonet. And when the smoke cleared, the burden of loss and the effort to rebuild fell not only on famous names, but on every family, neighbor, and friend.

Throughout these pages, I have worked to bring you as many voices as possible. The story of Lexington and Concord is not the property of any one group. It belongs as much to the British rank-and-file as to the colonial militia. It belongs to the Loyalists forced to choose between country and home. It belongs to women like Mary Barrett, Ruth Harrington, and Sarah Estabrook, whose determination and resilience shaped their communities. It belongs to Black participants such as Prince Estabrook, whose names too often faded from commemoration. By weaving these perspectives together, we gain a fuller, truer understanding of what happened and why it matters.

Along the way, we confronted the myths that have grown up around these events. The lone ride of Paul Revere, the cry "The British are coming!" and the famous "shot heard 'round the world" have become touchstones of American identity. Yet, as you have seen, these tales often simplify or distort the real complexity. Through firsthand accounts, maps, timelines, and careful analysis, I hope you now see both the power and the limits of legend. My aim is not to strip away inspiration, but to ground it in the courage, fear, and confusion that real people felt. This makes their choices all the more meaningful.

The legacy of April 19, 1775, endures. In the days and weeks that followed, communities mourned, rebuilt, and debated. News of Lexington and Concord swept across the colonies, stirring unity and resistance. Over generations, these events became symbols—commemorated in parades, monuments, and classroom lessons. Yet the memory of that day has never been static. Each generation retells the story, shaping it to fit its own questions and needs. Today, the fields, taverns, and bridges of Lexington and Concord remain living classrooms. They remind us that liberty is not an abstract ideal, but the product of countless small decisions—of neighbors answering alarms, of families enduring loss, of communities choosing to stand together in uncertainty.

I have tried to make this book a practical companion for all who seek to understand and remember. You have seen clear maps and timelines to track the action, firsthand accounts that put you in the shoes of those who were there, and site guides for walking the ground yourself. Myth-busting sidebars have offered tools for separating fact from fiction. Whether you are a student, a teacher, a traveler, or a lifelong reader of history, I hope these resources have given you confidence to explore further, to question, and to interpret for yourself.

The story does not end on the final page. I urge you to visit these sites if you can—walk Lexington Green at sunrise, linger at North Bridge, explore Minute Man National Historical Park, or follow the Battle Road Trail. Seek out original documents in libraries and museums. Join a walking tour, attend a reenactment, or simply pause before a monument to consider what it represents. Ask questions, share what you have learned, and invite others to join the conversation. History belongs to those who care enough to keep it alive.

Most of all, I invite you to reflect on the choices made in 1775. The men and women of Lexington and Concord faced uncertainty, danger, and the unknown. They did not know if liberty could be won, or what it would cost. Yet they acted—sometimes in confusion, often in fear, but always with a sense of responsibility to their neighbors and their own ideals. In our own time, we too face challenges that demand courage, reflection, and community. The lessons of April 19 are not only for museums or textbooks. They speak to every moment when ordinary people are called to make difficult choices, to stand together, and to shape the future they wish to see.

As someone who cares deeply about bringing clarity and honesty to American history, I thank you for joining me on this journey. My hope is that you leave these pages empowered—not only to understand what happened at Lexington and Concord, but to discuss, question, and share these stories with others. The Revolution began not with certainty, but with the willingness to act in the face of doubt. That spirit remains our inheritance. May we honor it, not only by remembering, but by continuing to learn, explore, and strive together for the promise of freedom.

Thank you for completing this book.

I hope its contents meant a lot to you. As I mentioned earlier, when you can, please spend just a little time writing a review of *Lexington and Concord: The First Shots of Freedom*

Many potential readers consider the quality and quantity of reviews a book has earned, and the better the reviews, the more a seller prioritizes it.

All you have to do is locate this book online, scroll down to where it says "Write a customer review," and follow the directions to write a much-appreciated review. It doesn't have to be long. They recommend at least a few sentences.

Thanks much in advance.

Please keep reading,

Blake Whitworth

References

- The Coming of the American Revolution: 1764 to 1776 https://www.masshist.org/revolution/
- Powder Alarm, 1774, American Revolution, Summary, Facts https://www.americanhistorycentral.com/entries/powder-alarm-1774-massachusetts/
- Boston Committee of Correspondence records - NYPL Archives https://archives.nypl.org/mss/343
- What are Minutemen? | T H Bell Junior High https://thbell.wsd.net/o/thbjh/page/what-are-minutemen
- Interactive Map: The Midnight Rides https://www.paulreverehouse.org/interactive-map-midnight-rides/
- A Network of Midnight Riders Alert the Countryside https://www.battlefields.org/learn/articles/spread-alarm-network-midnight-riders-alert-countryside
- Orders to Lieut. Colonel Smith, 10th Regiment 'Foot https://teachingamericanhistory.org/document/orders-from-general-thomas-gage-to-lieut-colonel-smith-10th-regiment-foot/
- Who was Maj. Gen. Dr. Joseph Warren? (1741 - 1775) https://www.wchsmuseum.org/josephwarren.html

- April 19, 1775 - Minute Man National Historical Park (U.S.
- https://www.nps.gov/mima/learn/historyculture/april-19-1775.htm
- Deposition of Captain John Parker Concerning the Battle at. https://docsteach.org/document/john-parker-lexington/
- The Loyalist Guides of Lexington and Concord https://allthingsliberty.com/2016/05/the-loyalist-guides-of-lexington-and-concord/
- Prince Estabrook of Lexington (U.S. National Park Service) https://www.nps.gov/people/prince-estabrook-of-lexington.htm
- A Deposition of Colonial Militiamen from the Battle. https://www.battlefields.org/learn/primary-sources/deposition-colonial-militiamen-battle-lexington-and-concord
- John Parker https://www.battlefields.org/learn/biographies/john-parker
- Battles of Lexington and Concord https://en.wikipedia.org/wiki/Battles_of_Lexington_and_Concord
- April 19, 1775 - Minute Man National Historical Park (U.S. https://www.nps.gov/mima/learn/historyculture/april-19-1775.htm
- A Deposition of Colonial Militiamen from the Battle. https://www.battlefields.org/learn/primary-

sources/deposition-colonial-militiamen-battle-lexington-and-concord

- Lexington and Concord | British Retreat | Apr 18-19, 1775
  https://www.battlefields.org/learn/maps/battle-lexington-and-concord-british-retreat-april-18-19-1775
- North Bridge: First Forcible Resistance to the British Advance
  https://www.battlefields.org/learn/articles/north-bridge-first-forcible-resistance-british-advance
- The Civilian Evacuation of April 19, 1775
  https://www.discoverconcordma.com/articles/119-the-civilian-evacuation-of-april-19-1775
- Battle Road: "To Attack and Annoy the Enemy"
  https://www.battlefields.org/learn/primary-sources/battle-road-attack-and-annoy-enemy
- The Battle of Menotomy | Arlington Historical Society
  https://arlingtonhistorical.org/learn/articles/the-battle-of-menotomy/
- April 19, 1775 - Minute Man National Historical Park (U.S.
  https://www.nps.gov/mima/learn/historyculture/april-19-1775.htm
- A Turn for the Worse: The 1775 Ambush at Bloody Angle https://www.historynet.com/a-turn-for-the-worse-the-1775-ambush-at-bloody-angle/

- April 19, 1775 - Minute Man National Historical Park (U.S. https://www.nps.gov/mima/learn/historyculture/april-19-1775.htm
- Women and The Battle of Lexington and Concord https://www.battlefields.org/learn/articles/women-and-battle-lexington-and-concord
- The Plight of Massachusetts Loyalists https://www.americanheritage.com/plight-massachusetts-loyalists
- "Forever Bear In Mind:" Spreading the News of Lexington ... https://www.readex.com/readex-report/issues/volume-4-issue-4/forever-bear-mind-spreading-news-lexington-and-concord
- The Battle Road Trail - Minute Man National Historical. https://www.nps.gov/mima/planyourvisit/the-battle-road-trail.htm
- History & Culture - Minute Man National Historical Park. https://www.nps.gov/mima/learn/historyculture/index.htm
- April 19, 1775 Witness Houses - Minute Man. https://www.nps.gov/mima/learn/historyculture/april-19-1775-witness-houses.htm
- The Shot Heard Round the World: April 19, 1775 https://concordmuseum.org/online-exhibition/the-shot-heard-round-the-world-april-19-1775/

www.ingramcontent.com/pod-product-compliance
Lightning Source LLC
LaVergne TN
LVHW051408080426
835508LV00022B/2982